Hope
For Your Journey

Hope
FOR YOUR JOURNEY

DIANNE TOLLIVER

XULON PRESS

Xulon Press
555 Winderley Pl, Suite 225
Maitland, FL 32751
407.339.4217
www.xulonpress.com

© 2024 by Revitalize Now, LLC

All rights reserved solely by the author. The author guarantees all contents are original and do not infringe upon the legal rights of any other person or work. No part of this book may be reproduced in any form without the permission of the author.

Due to the changing nature of the Internet, if there are any web addresses, links, or URLs included in this manuscript, these may have been altered and may no longer be accessible. The views and opinions shared in this book belong solely to the author and do not necessarily reflect those of the publisher. The publisher therefore disclaims responsibility for the views or opinions expressed within the work.

Unless otherwise indicated, Scripture quotations taken from the English Standard Version (ESV). Copyright © 2001 by Crossway, a publishing ministry of Good News Publishers. Used by permission. All rights reserved.

Unless otherwise indicated, Scripture quotations taken from the Holy Bible, New International Version (NIV). Copyright © 1973, 1978, 1984, 2011 by Biblica, Inc.™. Used by permission. All rights reserved.

Unless otherwise indicated, Scripture quotations taken from the New King James Version (NKJV). Copyright © 1982 by Thomas Nelson, Inc. Used by permission. All rights reserved.

Unless otherwise indicated, Scripture quotations taken from the King James Version (KJV) – *public domain*.

Unless otherwise indicated, Scripture quotations taken from The Message (MSG). Copyright © 1993, 1994, 1995, 1996, 2000, 2001, 2002. Used by permission of NavPress Publishing Group. Used by permission. All rights reserved

Paperback ISBN-13: 979-8-86850-240-8
Dust Jacket ISBN-13: 979-8-86850-241-5
Ebook ISBN-13: 979-8-86850-242-2

Dedication

To the remarkable people who courageously
shared their personal and inspirational stories
to make this book a reality.

A Special Note of Appreciation

The following people provided invaluable support
and encouragement during this book journey.
Thank you!

Michele Bruce
Barbara Butler
Brooke Campbell
Scott Campbell
Jonny Coleman
Dr. Rob Coleman
Mark Connel
Bunni Cooper
Bev Ewbank
Gina Ferrell
Corrine Gormont
Bev Hayes
Claudia Rusnak
Larry Trammell

Contents

Introduction xi

Engulfed in Flames xiii

The Blessings of Adoption 11

Protected by God 23

Rebuilding Your Marriage with God 30

An Immigrant's Faith 42

Appearances Can Be Deceiving 57

Overcoming An Opioid Dependency 65

The Freedom Honor Flight 77

Choosing Faith Over Fear 81

Surviving Pancreatic Cancer 94

Surrounded by Wildfires 104

The Family I Never Knew 111

Pause and Reflect 123

A Wild Teenager – But God Had a Plan! 127

God Comforts Us Through Others 145

A Weight Loss Journey – And So Much More 157

Touching Lives Through Teaching 168

The Power of a Simple Apology and Forgiveness 178

Pay It Forward 186

Take Time to Re-Energize 190

A Final Reflection 197

Three Steps to Salvation 199

Introduction

In the blink of an eye, life drastically changed when COVID invaded our world. During the darkest days of the pandemic, we grieved for strangers and ached for families who lost loved ones. Doctors, nurses, and first responders became our heroes as hugging a friend became a significant health risk. The world as we knew it suddenly turned upside down.

As the pandemic raged, businesses and schools closed while unemployment surged. Massive hurricanes plummeted our coasts, and hundreds of wildfires scorched the west. Social divisions deepened as political and civil unrest filled the streets. Peace eluded our society.

Then COVID and unemployment hit my family. Despite my fears, I chose to place my trust in God. I knew He would not leave me; He would not leave my family. Yes, there were discouraging and hard days, but as I looked to our Heavenly Father for comfort, He revealed the blessings in my life. My heart became full of love, peace, and gratitude.

Thankfully, family members recovered from COVID. We still had a roof over our heads and food on our table. Birds were singing in the trees, and deer gathered in the backyard. Our "Zoom Events" with family and friends turned into heartwarming experiences full of laughter and encouragement. Car parades to celebrate birthdays and graduations became unique gifts of love. As it turned out, slowing down and living a "simpler" life was also a blessing.

As the pandemic finally began to slow down, I asked God for guidance regarding my next steps. What did He want me to do? After months of prayer, it was clear that I should write a third book, "Hope for Your Journey." For with God, there is ALWAYS HOPE. He will faithfully light your path.

The resulting true stories, captured in the pages ahead, share the unplanned journeys of my friends, family, and acquaintances. The

Hope For Your Journey

stories provide an unfiltered glimpse into their joys, challenges, and heartbreaks while revealing God's love, compassion, and strength. Due to sensitive topics and for privacy protection, some names were changed in the stories. Each chapter concludes with thought-provoking questions to provide a time for personal reflection.

I pray the stories contained in this book provide "hope for your journey." As you trust God, He will sustain you – despite your circumstances or challenges. Choose to live your life in the light of our Heavenly Father. Embrace His promises today and every day.

"May the God of hope fill you with all
joy and peace as you trust in him,
so that you may overflow with hope
by the power of the Holy Spirit."
Romans 15:13 (NIV)

Blessings, Dianne

Engulfed In Flames

*"Yea, though I walk through
the valley of the shadow of death,
I will fear no evil: for thou art with me."
Psalm 23:4 (KJV)*

Within seconds, the hallway exploded in flames. As adrenaline took control, Police Officer Needels dove head-first down the stairs. Two officers quickly grabbed him and rushed out of the building. They were under attack!

Steve Needels grew up in a loving family devoted to God, country, and respect for others. Integrity and ethics were a cornerstone of his upbringing. His Father served in the military and law enforcement, while his mother was a pillar of strength, always encouraging and loving others.

While growing up, Steve considered a call to the ministry. Subsequently, after high school, he enrolled in Mount Vernon Nazarene College to explore this path. However, as semesters passed, it became clear Steve had a passion for Wall Street, which was a definite turn in his journey. So, he changed his major to pursue a banking career. Yet, during this time, he quietly yearned to become a police officer.

In 1988, Steve graduated from college and launched his successful banking career. He soon married his girlfriend Melanie, and by 1992, he was a bank manager. Life was going great.

Yet, this yearning to become a police officer distracted Steve's thoughts. Finally, after months of prayer and many discussions with his wife, he quit his job to pursue a career in law enforcement while Melanie continued her profession as a school teacher.

Steve graduated from the Fairfax Police Academy in 1993, then accepted a position as a patrol officer at the McLean District Station in Northern Virginia. Steve and Melanie understood the daily risks

Hope For Your Journey

associated with a career in law enforcement but did not allow fear to impact their relationship or day-to-day activities. They placed Steve in God's hands and moved forward with their lives.

"So do not fear, for I am with you;
do not be dismayed, for I am your God.
I will strengthen you and help you;
I will uphold you with my righteous right hand."
Isaiah 41:10 (NIV)

Then, one typical morning in May 1995, Steve reported to roll call at 5:30 AM. He jumped into his police cruiser and hit the streets, unsure how the day would unfold.

Around 11 AM, the U.S. Secret Service intercepted a call to the White House — a man threatened the life of President George H. W. Bush. Secret Service agents quickly tracked the call to an apartment complex in Northern Virginia, about twenty minutes from the White House. They immediately contacted the local police department and requested they send officers to assess the situation.

Steve and two other officers received dispatch orders with the corresponding address. Upon arrival, the officers entered the complex wearing bulletproof vests. They ran up the stairs to the second floor, carefully following proper protocol.

Since Steve was the senior police officer, he identified the correct apartment number and approached the door. He could hear some commotion inside the apartment. With his back against the adjacent door, he leaned over and knocked on the suspect's door with his right hand.

No one responded. It was suddenly quiet. Steve waited a minute, knocked again, and identified himself as a police officer. Slowly, the door opened. A safety chain was still latched to the wall, only allowing a four-inch opening. Steve could not see anyone but noticed a person's shadow through the door hinges — someone was standing behind the door. With a firm voice, he asked the suspect to come out in the hallway to talk.

Then, he saw a man approaching the door carrying a yellow bucket — perhaps full of soapy water? Instantly, his God-given instincts kicked in as he leaned back from the door and thought, "Something's not right."

"God is our refuge and strength,
an ever-present help in trouble."
Psalm 46:1 (NIV)

In a split second, the man hurled the liquid into the hallway. The fluid splashed as it hit the floor, dousing Steve's arms, legs, and under his right eye. He felt an immediate burning sensation. Then, the hallway suddenly exploded in flames.

"The thief comes only to steal and kill and destroy..."
John 10:10 (NIV)

As adrenaline took control, Steve dove head-first down the stairs and landed flat on his back. The two officers grabbed him and rushed out of the building. They ran for cover behind the patrol cars as their eyes adjusted to the daylight.

Steve could hear sirens in the distance and knew help was on the way. He was relieved. He quickly assumed an offensive position as a police officer handed him a shotgun.

When he grabbed the gun, Steve noticed the skin on his right hand and arm was literally falling off his body. He immediately slipped into shock as the adrenaline from "survival mode" was replaced with intense pain from his severe burn injuries.

Steve has memory gaps due to his horrific pain. He remembers the emergency medical technicians (EMTs) loading him into the ambulance. He also recalls the shocking realization that his shirt and pants were missing due to the fire burning them off his body. Somehow, as Steve moved in and out of consciousness, he gave detectives his wife's name (Melanie) and the elementary school where she taught second grade.

As the ambulance doors closed, they rushed him to the local trauma center, but his second and third-degree burns were too significant for their trauma unit. Due to the high probability of infection, a medivac immediately flew Steve to the Washington Hospital Burn Center.

"...Do not let your hearts be troubled
and do not be afraid."
John 14:27 (NIV)

Hope For Your Journey

While doctors rushed to save Steve's life, police detectives contacted Melanie's school principal and informed her of the situation. For Melanie, it was a typical school day, and she had just sat down to have lunch. Suddenly, the principal entered the teachers' lounge – something she never did. Melanie thought it was odd.

She looked at Melanie and said, "I need to talk with you." Startled, Melanie got up and joined her as they found a private place to talk. The principal then shared, "Your husband was hurt. He knew your name and where you work." As Melanie intently listened, she thought, "OK – He can talk. He's alive."

> *"...In this world you will have trouble.*
> *But take heart! I have overcome the world."*
> *John 16:33 (NIV)*

The principal continued, "Some detectives are coming to pick you up. Go gather your things." Shocked but oddly calm, Melanie quietly prayed for Steve as she picked up her lunch, packed her teacher bag, and went to the school office.

Two detectives picked Melanie up in an unmarked car. It was a quiet ride to the hospital, with the officers providing few details about Steve's situation. Melanie was confused when they drove to the Washington Hospital versus the local hospital. She was alarmed when they informed her that a medivac helicopter had flown Steve to the Burn Center.

As they parked the car, one detective said, "There is press. We recommend you not talk to them – a bad guy is still at large." Melanie was unaware that the story about Steve was all over the television, including the local and national news. They quickly slid into the E.R., using a back door.

Melanie was allowed to see her husband once she washed her hands and put a sanitized gown over her clothes. When she entered the room, Steve was lying on a gurney. Due to flash burns, his face and body were completely gray. It was shocking. She could see a few bandages covering some of his burns.

When Steve looked up and saw Melanie, he started to cry and said, "I'm sorry." Melanie fought back tears. She was thankful he was alive and had an unexplainable sense of peace about Steve's situation. She knew

Engulfed In Flames

he was in God's hands as they embarked on this unexpected journey. They were not alone!

Soon after her visit, the surgical team sedated Steve and began the slow and painful process of removing burned skin from his arms, hands, and legs. The risk of infection was extremely high. The doctors needed to stabilize Steve's situation ASAP. Thankfully, the bulletproof vest protected his chest and back from the flames – providing healthy skin for future skin grafts.

As the hours passed, Melanie was grateful for the outpouring of love surrounding them. Steve's father was a pillar of strength as over fifty people, including pastors, family, police officers, and church members quietly gathered at the hospital to offer support and pray. Through the love and caring of others, God sustained and strengthened Steve and Melanie.

"Carry each other's burdens,
and in this way you will fulfill the law of Christ."
Galatians 6:2 (NIV)

During this waiting time, they learned some details about Steve's attack. The man at the apartment complex threw a bucket of gasoline into the hallway and onto Steve. He then lit a roll of paper towels and threw it into the gasoline-drenched hallway. The fire department extinguished the fire, and no one else was injured. Somehow, the assailant escaped. An active search was still underway.

After several hours, Steve's doctor emerged from the operating room to talk with Melanie. The doctor, whom she called Dr. Doom, was not optimistic. He said, "Steve might die tonight. He has second and third-degree burns over 33% of his body. He is in very serious condition. If he survives, Steve will remain in the intensive care unit (ICU) for several weeks." Despite hearing these words, Melanie felt God's peace about Steve's situation.

"And the peace of God, which transcends
all understanding, will guard your hearts
and your minds in Christ Jesus."
Philippians 4:7 (NIV)

That night, Melanie was allowed to visit Steve in the ICU. She was shocked to see his entire body wrapped in bandages with only small openings for his eyes. He was heavily sedated and unresponsive as they strived to keep his intense pain under control. Her twenty-nine-year-old husband looked like a mummy. It was a sobering sight.

As Steve fought for his life, Melanie held on to her faith while friends, family, and strangers prayed for his complete healing. Despite his grave situation, she continued to believe everything would be OK.

> *"But when you ask, you must believe and not doubt,*
> *because the one who doubts*
> *is like a wave of the sea,*
> *blown and tossed by the wind."*
> *James 1:6 (NIV)*

Due to the risk of infection, she could not spend the night in Steve's room. Melanie was exhausted, so her parents took her home to get some rest. Thankfully, some police officers drove her car from the school to their house. She was grateful.

The following morning, before heading to the hospital, Melanie's father asked for the name of Steve's attacker. Then, in Christian love, he prayed out loud for Steve's complete healing. Next, by name, her Father prayed for the man who set Steve on fire. He asked God to help them forgive this man and give them peace over the following weeks and months.

Melanie shared, "My father's prayer that morning shocked me. However, it kick-started my long journey with God to eventually forgive the man who caused Steve's horrific injuries and pain."

> *"But if you do not forgive others their sins,*
> *your Father will not forgive your sins."*
> *Matthew 6:15 (NIV)*

God encircled Melanie with a miraculous sense of peace as she drove to the hospital that morning, not knowing how the day would unfold. She kept trusting God and leaning on Him for strength. She knew God would carry Steve through this horrible situation.

Upon arrival at the ICU, Melanie only had a few minutes with Steve due to his horrific pain. She did her best to encourage him as he drifted in and out of consciousness. Then Steve quietly said, "I don't want to sit behind a desk."

Engulfed In Flames

Melanie's heart broke when she heard his comment, but she also understood her husband and his work ethic. He believed, "With God, all things are possible. If you get knocked down, get back up and keep going." She knew he was motivated to recover and return to the streets as a police officer.

Melanie decided sitting in the hospital waiting room would not help anyone. So, she hopped in her car and drove to school. Given Steve's situation, the teachers and students were stunned to see her, but her visit was therapeutic for all of them. Melanie had God-inspired, hopeful conversations with the staff and students before returning to the hospital.

That same day, the police apprehended Steve's attacker. The Virginia Commonwealth Attorney charged the assailant with attempted capital murder and malicious burning. His capture relieved the entire family, but Steve faced a long road to recovery.

As the days passed, Steve continued to suffer from his horrific burns. The daily wound cleanings and bandage changes were extremely painful. Despite his situation, he continued to trust God and lean on Him for strength.

"Have mercy on me, Lord, for I am faint;
heal me, Lord, for my bones are in agony.
My soul is in deep anguish.
How long, Lord, how long?"
Psalm 6:2-3 (NIV)

Steve shared, "Then, early one morning, as I laid in the hospital bed covered in bandages, I sensed things would work out – I was suddenly at peace. I knew God was with me."

He endured two painful skin graft surgeries as part of his recovery. The doctors carefully removed healthy skin from his chest and transplanted it to his left hand and leg. His leg required significant grafting due to the deep burns.

Steve's face, ears, and lips soon turned black from the flash burns – but no surgical procedures were required. The doctors were optimistic this skin would naturally heal over several months.

Hope For Your Journey

While Steve remained in the ICU, Melanie returned to the classroom, teaching half days. She would go to the hospital in the morning, teach part of the day, then return to the hospital. Melanie was grateful for the unwavering support from her principal, teaching staff, and students. She shared, "When I drove to and from the hospital, I would sing praise songs to the Lord. God helped me find joy in the middle of our storm."

"Be joyful in hope, patient in affliction,
faithful in prayer."
Romans 12:12 (NIV)

The continued outpouring of love, support, and prayers from friends and the community was overwhelming. They received boxes of letters and notes that were full of encouragement and uplifting thoughts. Even the school kids wrote letters to Officer Needels. They read every letter and card. They were grateful.

Then, one day, a stranger walked into the hospital and handed Melanie an envelope that contained hundreds of dollars. The man briefly shared that he was a "burn survivor" and understood what they were going through. He wanted to help. Without giving his name, he turned around and left the hospital. They never saw him again. He was a blessing from God!

After eighteen days in the ICU, Steve wanted to go home. His skin grafts were successful, he was regaining strength, and his pain levels were under control. So, the doctors discharged Steve, providing Melanie agreed to follow the "anti-infection" protocols and change his bandages twice each day.

"The Lord sustains them on their sickbed
and restores them from their bed of illness."
Psalm 41:3 (NIV)

As his recovery continued at home, Steve received regular physical therapy. The doctors were concerned that he could not bend his left leg due to the skin grafts. Steve worked hard and finally regained his leg's full range of motion.

Miraculously, Steve resumed work on August 18th, just fifteen weeks after the fire. He was not confined to desk work but returned to the streets as a police officer with no limitations. God was faithful once again.

In January of the following year, the man who engulfed Steve in flames was found guilty of attempted capital murder and malicious burning. The jury that convicted him recommended thirty years in prison. Steve was required to testify at the trial. He simply stated the facts, leaving the outcome to the jury.

As a result of his faith and reliance on God, Steve never became angry at the man who burned him. He said, "If I allowed myself to become angry, the adversary would win twice. Because of my faith, I accepted what happened to me and moved on. God gave me peace about the situation. I am grateful."

"Do not repay anyone evil for evil.
Be careful to do what is right in the eyes of everyone.
If it is possible, as far as it depends on you,
live at peace with everyone."
Romans 12:17-18 (NIV)

Two years later, Steve and Melanie celebrated the birth of their son, Austin. Over the years, their son has been a true blessing and a constant reminder that all things are possible with God. Austin and his wife Julia continue to fill their lives with joy, fun, and laughter.

Steve's law enforcement career spanned over twenty-eight years before his retirement. After serving as a patrol officer, he was a detective for the retail and thefts division, then an undercover detective for the narcotics division. Later, he became a detective in the Major Crimes Bureau, focusing on auto thefts, robberies, and homicides. Throughout his career, he was honored to mentor others.

Melanie and Steve recently celebrated their thirty-fourth anniversary and are active in their local church. They enjoy traveling and spending time with family and friends. They truly understand and embrace the gift of life.

In closing, Steve has many physical scars from the burns, but his heart and soul are stronger than ever. Based on Psalm 23:4, he now has a tattoo that says, "FEAR NO EVIL."

Praise God!

Steve before the fire.

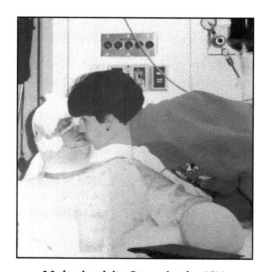

Melanie visits Steve in the ICU. Due to his extensive burns, bandages cover his entire body.

Engulfed In Flames

REFLECTION

We live in a fallen world. Unfortunately, bad things happen to good people. Thankfully, with God's help, Steve and Melanie:

- Chose to embrace peace versus fear.
- Chose to embrace forgiveness versus anger.
- Chose to live in God's love and light versus the adversary's world of darkness and bitterness.

How are you <u>choosing</u> to live your life?

_____

_____

_____

_____

_____

_____

_____

_____

_____

_____

_____

_____

_____

_____

_____

_____

Hope For Your Journey

NEXT STEPS

1. Take a moment and do some soul-searching.

   - Are you struggling to forgive someone today? If yes, who?

   _____

   _____

   - Are you angry?

   _____

   _____

   - Are you afraid? What are you afraid of?

   _____

   _____

2. There is good news.

   God will meet you right where you are and help you. You can pray the simple prayers below:

   Dear God,
   - I am struggling to forgive _____. Please help me.
   - I am tired of being angry at _____. Please help me.
   - I am afraid of _____. Please help me.

   Thank you. Amen.

CLOSING PRAYER

Dear Heavenly Father,

Thank you for carrying me through my challenges, fears, and adversities. Thank you for caring about my small and big issues. I am SO grateful.

I love you. Amen.

The Blessings of Adoption

"I prayed for this child, and the Lord
has granted me what I asked of him."
1 Samuel 1:27 (NIV)

A few weeks before the final adoption hearing, Vladimir Putin (the President of Russia) suddenly stopped all adoptions between Russia and the United States. As heightened political tensions between the two countries intensified, Dawn-Marie cried out to God, "Lord, please help me. This sweet child has already called me Mama."

Dawn-Marie's journey to pursue an international adoption began several years earlier. As a United Methodist Minister, she loved serving the Lord, leading churches, and helping people. While her life was overflowing with blessings, she longed to get married and have children. Unfortunately, as time passed, the dream of having a family eluded her. Dawn-Marie said, "Most men are not interested in becoming a pastor's husband." So, being a realist, she openly shared, "If I am not married by the age of forty, I am going to adopt a child."

By the age of thirty-eight, her desire to become a mother intensified. She now owned a home, but it was void of children. Being a firm believer in the power of prayer, Dawn-Marie began to pray for God's will regarding the possibility of adopting a child.

"Do not be anxious about anything, but in every situation,
by prayer and petition, with thanksgiving,
present your requests to God."
Philippians 4:6 (NIV)

During this same time, there were challenges at the church where she served as a lead pastor. She said, "In retrospect, my hardest years in ministry became one of my greatest blessings. God used my challenges to transition me to another church and open new doors."

As Dawn-Marie prepared to move to a different church and city, her realtor placed a "For Sale" sign in her front yard. Shockingly, her home sold for a price that was significantly over her original purchase price. She was stunned and praised God for this unexpected blessing.

Dawn-Marie was unaware that through the sale of her home, God faithfully provided the money she would need for her future international adoption, including lawyer payments, fees, and travel expenses. God was in control – this was just the first of several miracles He would perform during her adoption journey.

When she arrived at her new church, Dawn-Marie became friends with a couple who had recently adopted a child from China. She knew God created this connection. The couple openly shared their adoption journey and how they maneuvered through the U.S. and international legal processes. They became a source of encouragement and support.

Over the next several months, she faithfully prayed and asked for God's guidance and direction regarding an adoption. During one particular prayer time, God reminded Dawn-Marie about a unique Russian ornament she received from her parents when she was only eight years old. In that time of reflection, God "placed on her heart" that her future child should come from Russia.

"The Lord watches over the foreigner and sustains the fatherless…"
Psalm 146:9 (NIV)

With that "ah-ha" realization, she began researching various international adoption organizations. After months of research and prayers, she trusted God and connected with a reputable Christian adoption agency in Northern Virginia. Finally, when the time felt right, Dawn-Marie completed and notarized the extensive paperwork required to adopt a child from Russia. She requested an infant between one and twenty months old.

The complex process required "pay as you go" fees, with no guarantee that an adoption would occur. Dawn-Marie had done all she could – her future and potential child was now in the Lord's hands. All she could do was hope and continue to pray.

"But those who hope in the Lord will renew their strength.
They will soar on wings like eagles;

they will run and not grow weary,
they will walk and not be faint."
Isaiah 40:31 (NIV)

Finally, after twenty-two long months, the phone rang! There was a possible referral to adopt a twenty-one-month-old child in Russia. Overwhelmed by the call, Dawn-Marie told the adoption office she would get back to them but needed a little time. She wanted to seek God's will for her next steps. When she shared the exciting news with her church friends, they prayed that Dawn-Marie would have clarity and know if this was the right adoption referral by the time she arrived home.

When Dawn-Marie opened the front door of her home, her heart and mind suddenly filled with an overwhelming assurance – this was the right adoption referral. She immediately called the adoption office and said YES!

She soon received a picture of an adorable little girl in a big yellow fluffy hat. Dawn-Marie lovingly studied the picture and thought, "Oh my goodness! She has my nose. God picked her for me."

"For I know the plans I have for you," declares the Lord,
"plans to prosper you and not to harm you,
plans to give you hope and a future."
Jeremiah 29:11 (NIV)

A bio accompanied the picture, stating the little girl's parents were alcoholics and relinquished all their rights to their daughter and walked away. There had been no follow-up contact. The bio also disclosed this little child had significant health challenges. She was born prematurely with fetal alcohol syndrome. She also had a heart ventricle issue, rickets, and fluid around her kidneys.

"Though my father and mother forsake me,
the Lord will receive me."
Psalm 27:10 (NIV)

While reading through the bio, Dawn-Marie realized this toddler was born around the same time she started the adoption process – this was NOT a random coincidence. God was in control of the situation! Despite the concerns documented in the report, she chose to keep trusting God and move forward.

> *"Trust in the Lord with all your heart*
> *and lean not on your own understanding;*
> *in all your ways submit to him,*
> *and he will make your paths straight."*
> *Proverbs 3:5-6 (NIV)*

The adoption process required Dawn-Marie to travel to Russia. Before leaving the U.S., she was instructed to put specific amounts of cash in envelopes and pay pre-coordinated people for their services as she maneuvered her way throughout Russia. It was scary, but she carefully followed the directions outlined by the adoption agency and prayed.

Dawn-Marie did not travel to Russia alone. A dear friend named Mindy accompanied her for moral support. Within a few weeks after the referral call, they boarded a nine-hour flight to Moscow. Thankfully, due to her pastoral connections, Dawn-Marie had friends who lived in Moscow. So, after their daunting process through Russian customs, they were grateful to see friends, enjoy a warm meal, and get a good night's rest before the next part of their journey.

The following morning, they boarded another plane for a four-hour flight to Kemerovo. Once in Kemerovo, a driver and translator met them for a ninety-minute drive to the orphanage, which was located in a small village out in the country. Dawn-Marie carefully passed the envelopes filled with cash to the specific people who provided support and prayed unceasingly every step of the way.

> *"Rejoice always, pray continually,*
> *give thanks in all circumstances..."*
> *1 Thessalonians 5:16-18 (NIV)*

It was cold and snowing when their car approached the huge, black iron-rod gates in front of the orphanage. Excitement and nerves filled Dawn-Marie's body as the gates slowly opened, and their car pulled up in front of a long, two-story brick building. When they entered the freshly painted building, they were met by one of the orphanage directors.

After a few pleasantries in Russian, the director escorted them to an office. Then, with the assistance of their interpreter, they reviewed the little girl's health issues. Hearing the health report in person was different than reading the bio. Dawn-Marie still had the option to change her mind if she did not want to go forward with the adoption.

The Blessings of Adoption

"Religion that God our Father accepts as pure and faultless is this:
to look after orphans and widows in their distress
and to keep oneself from being polluted by the world."
James 1:27 (NIV)

A few minutes later, an adorable, tiny, blond toddler dressed in a Donald Duck shirt and pink pants entered the office. She was holding hands with a woman from the orphanage. Prompted by God, Dawn-Marie immediately dropped to her knees and held her hands out. Without hesitation, little Daria ran into her arms. Dawn-Marie shared, "I instantly fell in love with this precious child of God."

After the emotional introduction, they moved to a cheery playroom painted pink and blue. It was full of toys and activities for the children. For the next two hours, they played together and danced to music from a boombox. They had fun! God filled the room with love, joy, and laughter.

Dawn-Marie shared, "Thanks to God, we emotionally bonded that afternoon despite our language barrier. As I held Daria in my arms, I still remember her fascination with fish and her little finger pushing against the fish tank in the playroom. I soaked up each moment since I was not allowed to take pictures. Pictures were only permitted after I signed the adoption paperwork."

Their allotted two-hour visit passed far too quickly. After hugging Daria goodbye, Dawn-Marie, Mindy, their interpreter, and the driver headed back to Kemerovo to spend the night. They were exhausted.

The following morning, Mindy gave Dawn-Marie a blue sweater vest as she prepared to take the next step in the adoption process. Despite Daria's health challenges, she met with a Russian notary and signed the official adoption paperwork before returning to the orphanage for another visit. She was "all in" as she fully trusted our Heavenly Father on her adoption journey.

"And whoever welcomes one such child
in my name welcomes me."
Matthew 18:5 (NIV)

That afternoon, Daria entered the orphanage playroom wearing a little blue dress that matched the color of Dawn-Marie's new vest. They chuckled at the "God Wink" as Daria walked toward her future Mom

Hope For Your Journey

without hesitation. Every step of their journey was God-filled, and they were grateful.

During this short visit, Dawn-Marie gave Daria a small photo album. They enjoyed looking at pictures of her family members, house, and cat. Each image was carefully labeled. When they finished looking through the book, Daria stood up and quietly went to a corner of the room. Dawn-Marie graciously gave her space and prayed.

A few minutes later, Daria crawled up to sit with her again. She pointed to Dawn-Marie, her picture in the album, and said, "Mama." Dawn-Marie started to cry, looked at Mindy, and then joyfully asked, "Did you hear that? She called me Mama." God's love filled the room. Through the interpreter, the orphanage workers declared, "This is meant to be!"

Dawn-Marie gave the orphanage director the notarized paperwork and signed additional papers to start the formal adoption process through the Russian courts. They took pictures, laughed, and gave last-minute hugs before returning to the hotel. It was a joyful day!

On the last day of their trip, they returned to the orphanage for a final visit before flying back to the U.S. Dawn-Marie gave Daria a little doll, which she gladly accepted. Everything at the orphanage was community property, so to have a new doll was extra special.

Mindy made a foam handprint of Daria's little hand – a thoughtful keepsake for Dawn-Marie to cherish and hold over the upcoming months. For you see, Daria had to remain in the orphanage while they waited for the Russian courts to set a formal date for the adoption proceedings. This process could take months.

The visit with Daria flew by, and it was once again time to leave. But this departure was different. Dawn-Marie had no idea when she would see Daria again. It broke her heart to say goodbye and leave her future daughter at the orphanage. Thankfully, with God's help, she remained strong until she got in the car and wept.

Over the following months, she kept busy with her church pastoral responsibilities while watching the calendar days pass by. She was grateful for friends, family, and church members who provided encouragement and support during this time. Dawn-Marie faithfully prayed

The Blessings of Adoption

for Daria's health, caregivers, and the adoption process. She firmly stood on God's promises and placed her hope in the Lord.

"Now faith is confidence in what we hope for
and assurance about what we do not see."
Hebrews 11:1 (NIV)

Finally, after months of waiting, she received a phone call from the adoption agency. The Russian courts finally set a date for Daria's adoption proceedings. Dawn-Marie was thrilled. Before boarding a plane to Russia, she had two short weeks to finalize her travel plans, fill the required envelopes with cash, and understand all the "legal hoops and next steps" provided by the adoption agency.

Then, an unexpected change in world politics took center stage in Dawn-Marie and Daria's lives. Vladimir Putin, the President of Russia, suddenly halted all adoptions between the United States and Russia. As heightened political tensions between the two countries intensified, Dawn-Marie's human mind feared she might lose Daria.

Thankfully, she firmly believed in the power of prayer and knew firsthand that ALL things are possible with God. So, she cried out, "Lord, I am afraid I will lose Daria. Please help me. This sweet child has already called me Mama."

"But when you ask, you must believe and not doubt,
because the one who doubts is like a wave of the sea,
blown and tossed by the wind."
James 1:6 (NIV)

God heard her cry for help. Suddenly, by the grace of God, Dawn-Marie received a "green light exception" to attend the scheduled court session due to Daria's pre-existing health issues. At the time, she did not fully grasp the significance of this exception, but it would become apparent as the months progressed.

As Dawn-Marie turned all her energy toward the adoption hearing, a long-time friend named Barbara accompanied her to Russia. They first flew to Moscow to handle several legal actions, then flew on to Kemerovo. Despite being in Kemerovo, only ninety minutes from the orphanage, Dawn-Marie was not allowed to see Daria before the court date.

Dawn-Marie prayed for strength and the court's approval on the morning of the final adoption hearing. When she arrived at the courthouse and walked through the cold hallways, the entire situation was intimidating. As she entered the courtroom and glanced around, she noticed a big table surrounded by a court stenographer, social worker, and interpreter. Barbara was not allowed in the room. The environment was serious and austere. There were no smiles. They all stood when a female judge entered the room and sat at the table. Amazingly, there were no men in the proceedings.

The adoption proceeding was in Russian. Through the interpreter, the judge asked several questions regarding family support as a single Mom, job security, etc. At one point, the judge requested that Dawn-Marie leave the room while they discussed the situation. She felt a high level of stress as she exited the room. So, as she had done throughout her life, she turned to God for strength and prayed, "Dear God, I know you gave me this child. I am trusting you."

"I prayed for this child,
and the Lord has granted me what I asked of him."
1 Samuel 1:27 (NIV)

After an unknown amount of time passed, they called her back into the room. Then, an amazing thing happened. The previously unemotional judge smiled at Dawn-Marie and spoke in Russian. The translator then shared her words in English, "Congratulations, you are a mom!" At that point, every woman in the courtroom smiled. God was in control! Amen!

The next few hours were a whirlwind as they quickly stopped by the hotel to get clothes for Daria since they could not take anything from the children's home. When they approached the orphanage, things looked different. It was now summer, and kids were running on the green grass. As she entered a gated area where the kids were playing, Daria looked up at Dawn-Marie, held her arms up, and said, "Mama!" God fulfilled Dawn-Marie's dream to become a mom!

Daria, Dawn-Marie, and Barbara stayed in a small Russian hotel room for the next two weeks. Numerous actions and additional paperwork were required before Daria could leave the country. Thankfully, the U.S. embassy and adoption agency helped coordinate the required physicals, dual citizenship, Russian and U.S. passports, etc. To honor God, during the dual-citizenship and passport process, Dawn-Marie officially changed Daria's first name to "Sarah-Grace" and kept Daria as her middle name. After all, it was through God's grace this adoption occurred.

But he said to me, "My grace is sufficient for you,
for my power is made perfect in weakness."
2 Corinthians 12:9 (NIV)

For Sarah-Grace, the transition to riding in cars, meeting new people, hearing new sounds, eating new food, and living in a hotel room was sometimes overwhelming. Thankfully, Dawn-Marie was in tune with her daughter's needs and fears. She quickly learned how to comfort her. Dawn-Marie used her sign language skills to communicate, in addition to lots of hugs and smiles.

Due to Sarah-Grace's documented medical issues, the Russian government granted a second "medical exception," which expedited their ability to fly back to the U.S. ten days earlier than expected. God was in control.

When they arrived in the U.S., they received another miracle. After numerous medical tests, the U.S. doctors determined Sarah-Grace did NOT have a heart ventricle issue, rickets, or fluid on her kidneys. Yet, those specific concerns allowed the "green light exception" for the adoption to proceed. God had intervened every step of the way.

Living in the U.S. for the past sixteen years, Sarah-Grace has blossomed into a beautiful teenager, full of love and hope. While she struggles with the effects of fetal alcohol syndrome, God and Dawn-Marie have been with her every step of the way. Sarah-Grace loves the Lord. When she faces challenges in school and anxiety due to the syndrome, she trusts God and His promises.

"I can do all this through Him who gives me strength."
Philippians 4:13 (NIV)

Dawn-Marie and Sarah-Grace enjoy a strong and unique bond. Each year, they celebrate "Gotcha Day," the official day they became mother and daughter. It is their special day, and they look forward to it every year. As part of their celebration, they always praise God. After all, HE is the reason they are together.

In closing, Dawn-Marie shared, "The year Sarah-Grace was born, there were approximately 5,000 U.S. / Russian adoptions. Once Putin stopped the adoption process, only six adoptions were allowed for a significant amount of time. Sarah-Grace's adoption was one of the six adoptions! God IS in the miracle business!"

She continued, "I praise and thank God daily for the privilege of being Sarah-Grace's Mom and Pastor. I can't imagine loving Sarah-Grace anymore — even if she was my biological daughter. I encourage anyone considering adoption to "go for it!" As our story shows, with God, ALL things are possible."

Dawn-Marie and Sarah-Grace　　　　**Sarah-Grace**

The Blessings of Adoption

REFLECTION

On a daily and sometimes minute-by-minute basis, Dawn-Marie sought God's guidance, strength, and intervention during her adoption journey. God was ALWAYS available and willing to help.

1. Can you recall the last time you talked to God?

_____

_____

_____

_____

_____

_____

_____

2. Can you recall the last time you listened to God?

_____

_____

_____

_____

_____

_____

_____

Hope For Your Journey

NEXT STEPS

Prayer is the most underutilized power in this world.

As we saw in this story, God is available 24/7 to listen to your requests, fears, and needs. You do not need fancy words or to be in a "special place" to pray. You can talk to your Heavenly Father anytime and anywhere, regardless of your past or current situation. You can pray out loud, silently in your head, or write your prayers on paper. Just be sincere with our Heavenly Father.

Some examples of ways to pray are below:

> Dear God,
> Thank you for loving me! I need some help.
> - Can you please help me _____?
> - I am afraid of _____. Please help me.
> - I need _____ so I can _____. Please help me.
> Amen.

CLOSING PRAYER

Dear Heavenly Father,

Thank you for being available to listen and help me 24/7. Thank you for caring about every part of my life! You are an AMAZING God, and I love you! Amen.

Protected By God

"The Lord is good,
a refuge in times of trouble.
He cares for those who trust in him,"
Nahum 1:7 (NIV)

It was a beautiful spring day in the Virginia countryside. Bev finished her coffee, hopped in her red convertible Mustang, and headed for the office. As she backed out of the driveway, she took a deep breath, then settled in for a ninety-minute drive to the city.

Bev didn't mind the long commute. It provided uninterrupted time to reflect on life, talk with God, and think about her upcoming day. She was grateful for this quiet time.

The first part of her trip was peaceful as she passed miles of open space and an occasional farm. The rolling, green fields were stunning, and the wildflowers were in full bloom. She was thankful for God's creations.

"But God made the earth by his power;
he founded the world by his wisdom
and stretched out the heavens
by his understanding."
Jeremiah 10:12 (NIV)

Before long, Bev began to approach the suburbs of Washington, DC. Traffic was lighter than expected, most likely due to the Memorial holiday earlier in the week. Regardless of the reason, she was pleased with her easier commute. She had no idea the light traffic would soon become a blessing.

As she rolled up to a stop light, Bev noticed a large dump truck on the left-hand side of the car. While waiting for the light to turn, the truck's spiked chrome hubcaps caught her attention. She thought, "Those wheel covers look dangerous. They must protect the truck. I've never noticed that type of hubcap and how the spikes stick out

Hope For Your Journey

from the wheel. How odd." A minute later, the light turned green, and Bev continued her drive to the office for a full day of meetings, or so she thought.

*"But the Lord is faithful, and he will
strengthen you and protect you from the evil one."
2 Thessalonians 3:3 (NIV)*

The truck's spiked hubcap.

As she merged onto the famous I-66, traffic was moving at a reasonable 65 MPH pace. Suddenly, in her right-hand mirror, she saw a fast-moving black car zooming down the onramp. It alarmed her.

Bev quickly assessed the vehicles around her Mustang. The lanes in front were full of cars, a huge gray dump truck filled with rocks and gravel was on her immediate left, and all four lanes behind her were full of cars. She was "boxed in."

Within a split second, the black car began to merge into her lane – heading directly for the right side of her car. The driver didn't see her. Bev's body filled with fear as she quickly thought, "Oh Lord, please take care of this. If this car hits me, many cars will crash – people will die."

*"When I am afraid, I put my trust in you."
Psalm 56:3 (NIV)*

Suddenly, the unfolding situation seemed to transition to slow motion. It was strange. Bev honked the horn as she swerved to the left, trying to avoid a collision. This maneuver placed her dangerously close to the truck on her left-hand side. Her window was only a foot away from the truck's chrome spiked hubcaps, oddly similar to the wheel covers she had noticed earlier in the morning.

Thankfully, the driver realized his mistake just before impact and made a quick correction. Bev's heart pounded as she caught her breath and thought, "Oh Lord, Thank You!"

"Cast all your anxiety on him
because he cares for you."
1 Peter 5:7 (NIV)

Unfortunately, the adversary was not done with Bev that morning. As she regained her composure from the scary incident, her low-riding car slipped into the dump truck's "blind spot." The truck could not see the Mustang and began merging into her lane.

Suddenly, one of the truck's spiked hubcaps collided with her car's left back wheel. Startled, Bev thought, "What's going on?" It happened quickly, and she was unable to counteract the impact. In a bizarre occurrence, the truck and Mustang were speeding down the highway at 65 MPH with connected wheels.

Bev's senses were immediately on "high alert" as adrenaline rushed throughout her body. The sound of grinding metal and the smell of shredding rubber permeated the car. Bev cried out, "Oh God, Help Me!" She knew He was the only way out of this dangerous situation.

"But when you ask, you must believe and not doubt,
because the one who doubts is like a wave of the sea,
blown and tossed by the wind."
James 1:6 (NIV)

Thoughts bombarded her mind as time seemed to transform into slow motion once again. As she glanced in her side mirror, she was perplexed. How were they connected? Then, for some odd reason, Bev recalled seeing the spiked hubcaps on this truck and quickly determined the spikes must have penetrated her tire and wheel well.

Hope For Your Journey

As her mind continued to process the situation, she held on to the steering wheel for dear life – struggling to keep the car straight while maintaining a steady speed. She feared the truck would lose control and roll on her car if she sped up, slowed down, or veered to the right or left.

"But you, Lord, do not be far from me.
You are my strength; come quickly to help me."
Psalm 22:19 (NIV)

As Bev briefly assessed the traffic around her, she worried several people would be injured if she crashed. But amazingly, as she glanced in the rearview mirror, no vehicles were directly behind her. The black car that nearly crashed into Bev a minute earlier sped up, and the right lane next to her car was now clear.

Within a split second, God made a straight, safe path for Bev to escape the potentially deadly situation. Bev knew she was in God's hands as she contemplated a way to disconnect from the truck. Time was of the essence.

"Trust in the Lord with all your heart
and lean not on your own understanding;
in all your ways submit to him,
and he will make your paths straight."
Proverbs 3:5-6 (NIV)

Bev then prayed, "God, please protect us. I'm going to pull my car off the spiked wheel." With that quick prayer, Bev firmly gripped the steering wheel and, with all her strength, slowly pulled the car to the right, realizing if she jerked too hard, the Mustang would flip, and the truck would spin out of control.

"God is our refuge and strength,
an ever-present help in trouble."
Psalm 46:1 (NIV)

With that maneuver, Bev separated from the spiked hubcap, but steering was difficult since the back tire was destroyed. Thankfully, with God's guiding hand, she safely pulled the car to the side of the road and stopped. As traffic sped by, she realized everyone was OK and thanked her Heavenly Father.

Protected By God

Bev watched as the truck safely stopped a few hundred feet in front of her car. The driver immediately jumped out of his vehicle and ran toward her. As Bev opened her car door, the truck driver ran up and embraced her, saying, "Thank God! Thank God you are OK!" They both burst into tears. It was a miracle they were unharmed.

Police soon arrived and classified the incident as a freak accident with a positive outcome; they issued no citations. Due to the significant damage to Bev's car, a tow truck hauled the Mustang to the repair shop, and her husband picked her up an hour later. As a result of the morning's unexpected events, she decided to skip work for the day. She thanked God for His miracles all the way home.

Bev shared, "I praise God for protecting so many people that morning. I was afraid, but God immediately helped me when I cried out. He provided an unexpected calmness during both incidents."

> *"I sought the Lord, and he heard me,*
> *and delivered me from all my fears."*
> *Psalm 34:4 (KJV)*

She continued, "It's a miracle God piqued my curiosity while sitting at the stoplight, allowing me to see the spiked hubcaps for the first time in my life. With that awareness and God's wisdom, I discerned the situation and figured out how to disconnect my car from the truck. Our Heavenly Father protected many lives that morning."

"When I looked in my rearview mirror and noticed no cars behind me, it felt like the parting of the Red Sea. The "sea of cars" seemed to disappear. I knew God was listening to me. I was grateful."

In closing, Bev said, "Remember, your Heavenly Father is always with you and ready to listen to your cries, fears, concerns, and praises. He loves you!"

Hope For Your Journey

REFLECTION

1. God protects us in big and small ways every single day. On this morning, only a few minutes before the traffic incidents, Bev saw a spiked hubcap for the first time in her life. God used that information to save many lives.

   Do you recall an incident in your life that you cannot explain from a worldly perspective? Did you remember to thank God for being with you during that situation?

   _____

   _____

   _____

   _____

   _____

2. Without hesitation, Bev cried out to God for help, not once but twice. She was in immediate danger but was confident her Heavenly Father would safely resolve her perilous dilemmas.

   Have you ever trusted God and asked Him to intervene and help you with a dilemma? If yes, what happened?

   _____

   _____

   _____

   _____

   _____

   _____

Protected By God

NEXT STEPS

God shows up when you call out to Him, but He wants to be part of your daily life.

Are you inviting God into your days and life, or do you only reach out when you need Him?

_____

_____

_____

_____

Do you want to change your current relationship with God? If yes, you can invite God into your days by praying this simple prayer:

> Dear Heavenly Father,
> I want to have a positive relationship with you. Please guide and direct my daily thoughts and decisions as I move forward. Amen.

CLOSING PRAYER

Dear Heavenly Father,

Thank you for being available 24/7. Please remind me to invite you into my daily life, not just when I need something. You are amazing. I love you. Amen.

Rebuilding Your Marriage with God

"But seek first his kingdom and his righteousness,
and all these things will be given to you as well."
Matthew 6:33 (NIV)

Kate was concerned. Something was different about her husband. After weeks of odd behavior, she finally asked him, "What's wrong?" He paused to look at her, then abruptly replied, "I'm leaving you." He then proceeded to pack his bags and move out that same evening. Kate was shocked and broken.

Mike and Kate first met through their local Baptist church youth group. Their families were active church members, so they saw each other regularly and became friends. As the years passed, Mike began dating Kate's best friend but secretly wanted to date Kate. Finally, during their senior year, Mike gathered the courage to ask Kate to the prom, and she said yes.

They continued to date after graduation and while attending the same Christian College. Unfortunately, they hit a "rough patch" during their freshman year and briefly broke up. Kate was heartbroken and hurt, but after a few months, they started to date again and became a tight couple. It was during this time Mike felt called to the ministry. He thought he would become a Christian counselor.

Toward the end of their sophomore year, the U.S. Government conducted the last draft for the Vietnam War, and Mike received a draft notice. Kate and Mike's plans for their future immediately changed. They were in love and knew they wanted to be together. So, after two years of college and many prayers, Mike signed up for the Navy. They both left college with plans to pursue their education sometime in the future. That same year, they were married in their hometown church by the music director, Pastor Smith – a pastor who would play a critical part in their lives many years later.

Rebuilding Your Marriage with God

After Mike's basic training, they moved into an apartment, started attending a great church, and began to enjoy married life together. Then, a few months after their marriage, they encountered a very dark time with their families. First, Kate's mother dealt with the emotional heartbreak of her father's continual infidelity. Then, Mike's father suddenly left his mother for a longtime mistress. Sadly, Mike's mother was so overwhelmed and distraught by her husband's actions she ended up in the hospital's psychiatric ward for assistance. The painful situations were overwhelming for the young married couple. They prayed for guidance and wisdom.

"Trust in the Lord with all your heart
and lean not on your own understanding;
in all your ways submit to him,
and he will make your paths straight."
Proverbs 3:5-6 (NIV)

Complicating the situation, Mike received orders to deploy on a ship right in the middle of their family upheaval. Due to his long deployment, he was concerned about Kate living alone without close friends or family nearby. So, he suggested Kate move back home to support her mother during his deployment. Kate reluctantly agreed to move, never realizing the painful future her mother would soon face.

While living with her mother, God blessed Kate with an unexpected career opportunity in the banking industry, a career that would provide many blessings in the future. When Mike returned from deployment, Kate moved again and promptly found another job. After Mike completed his three years of active duty, they moved back to their hometown and became actively involved in the same church where they were married. Mike sang in the choir, and they both taught Sunday School. Life was great!

Mike found a job and enrolled in the local university to finish his bachelor's degree in psychology, while Kate excelled in the banking industry. Before long, they purchased their first home. Then, they received the exciting news that Kate was pregnant. After five years of marriage, they welcomed a precious little boy named James into the world. They were living the American dream and felt very blessed.

Unfortunately, their lives took another unplanned turn when James was only three months old. Kate's mother, Mary, was diagnosed with advanced bone cancer. Due to the painful and debilitating disease,

Kate took a leave of absence from her job to care for her mom since her father continued to spend time with other women. Mike and Kate faithfully prayed that God would heal Mary and relieve her pain.

"Ask and it will be given to you; seek and you will find;
knock and the door will be opened to you.
For everyone who asks receives; the one who seeks finds;
and to the one who knocks, the door will be opened."
Matthew 7:7-8 (NIV)

Regrettably, Mary's health continued to deteriorate, and Mike struggled with his faith. He could not understand why God was not answering his prayers. After all, Mary was a good woman who constantly strived to live a model Christian life. Before long, he began to ask himself, "Where is God? Why isn't He healing Mary? As the days passed, Mike became increasingly disillusioned as his beloved mother-in-law died by inches. He felt God was letting him down.

After nine months of suffering, Mary passed away. Kate was heartbroken. Her father failed to provide emotional support and selfishly expanded his partying with other women. It was a painful time for Kate. She was sad and exhausted. So, she turned to her Heavenly Father for strength, then pressed forward, caring for their one-year-old son while returning to work.

"I can do all this through Him who gives me strength."
Philippians 4:13 (NIV)

On the other hand, Mary's death rocked Mike's foundation and beliefs. He was mad at God for not answering his prayers. In his confused state, he privately struggled with his feelings about God, failing to seek help from his wife, friends, or pastor. By himself and in the darkness, Mike quickly became an easy target for Satan.

"Be alert and of sober mind.
Your enemy the devil prowls around like a roaring lion
looking for someone to devour."
1 Peter 5:8 (NIV)

Sadly, due to his surface faith, Mike thought God was obligated to answer his prayers because he was doing good things for the church. He viewed his relationship with God from a worldly and transactional perspective. Mike could not see that God had answered his prayers,

Rebuilding Your Marriage with God

but not how he wanted. Mary's death (promotion to heaven) removed all her pain and healed her broken body. She was now with God.

Unfortunately, Satan was slithering around and did not miss the opportunity to prey on Mike's faltering state. The adversary started whispering, "Why are you going to church? Why are you tithing? Why are you being faithful to your wife?"

In a weakened state, Mike chose to walk away from God and the church to follow Satan's promptings. God gives us "free will" here on earth, and Mike decided to take the dark path. Yet, despite Mike's decision, God NEVER stopped loving or chasing after him.

"The thief comes only to steal and kill and destroy;
I have come that they may have life, and have it to the full."
John 10:10 (NIV)

Mike had an affair with a married woman. At first, Kate assumed he was attending church activities since he was involved with the children's ministry program. But, before long, she noticed his time away from home and odd behaviors centered around secrecy.

"But a man who commits adultery has no sense;
whoever does so destroys himself."
Proverbs 6:32 (NIV)

Finally, one evening, Kate blurted out, "What's wrong?" He paused to look at her, then abruptly replied, "I'm leaving you." He then packed his bags and moved out. Kate was shocked and heartbroken. She had never lived by herself and had a little boy. What was she going to do?

Mike moved in with his mother that evening. Thankfully, his mom immediately began to pray and never stopped. She prayed God would hold back the forces of evil long enough for him to wake up and make an intelligent decision. Then, one night, his mother had a dream. She saw Mike in a clergy robe – a vision she shared with him many years later.

When Pastor Smith, the man who married Mike and Kate, heard about their pending divorce, he immediately called Mike from his new church. First, he held Mike accountable for his unacceptable actions. Then, the pastor made two promises to him:

1. I will always love you no matter what you do.

2. I will always be there when you need me.

Out of love, he gave Mike a lifeline that would make a significant difference in the future. In addition, the pastor faithfully checked in on Mike over the following years, never allowing too much time to pass.

Sadly, the people in their church were uncomfortable with Kate and Mike's situation. As a result, some people ignored them, while others judged them at a time when they desperately needed love and support. The church's inability to walk with them during this painful time negatively impacted Mike and Kate. Then, one day, they told Kate she could not bring her son to the nursery because he was too hard to handle. As a result, Kate quit attending church and stopped adhering to some Christian values that were important to her.

"A new command I give you: Love one another.
As I have loved you, so you must love one another."
John 13:34 (NIV)

Toward the end of their divorce, Kate and Mike sold their home and divided their assets. Although Kate's world turned upside down due to no fault of her own, she still had a precious little boy, an excellent job with the bank, and Mike faithfully paid child support. After a short time, she purchased a townhome by herself. God provided a roommate who paid $150 a month, the exact amount she needed for a car payment. Our Heavenly Father never left Kate.

"Praise the Lord.
Give thanks to the Lord, for he is good;
His love endures forever."
Psalm 106:1 (NIV)

Mike soon moved into an old Victorian rental home and fully engaged in a party lifestyle. Sadly, he became an alcoholic and abandoned his goal to become a Christian counselor. However, despite his relentless partying, he kept his job as an insurance claim adjuster and fulfilled his responsibilities as a father. Kate openly told people that Mike was a good ex-husband. He faithfully paid child support and took James on weekends.

For the next four years, Mike and Kate dated various people and lived separate lives. However, they agreed to be respectful and cordial with each other for their son's well-being. They decided to celebrate special events as a family, including Thanksgiving, Christmas, and James' birthday. As a result, people would joke and say, "They are the friendliest exes we know."

Then, one night, when Mike was partying with a wild crowd, he was offered cocaine. When he asked for the price of the cocaine, the dealer said $65. Mike responded, "I can't pay that; I have to pay child support." To this day, Mike credits God and his mother's constant prayers for holding back the forces of evil that night.

Whether you turn to the right or to the left,
your ears will hear a voice behind you, saying,
"This is the way; walk in it."
Isaiah 30:21 (NIV)

When Mike was thirty-one, he experienced a life-altering event. He came home from a party late at night and was drunk as usual. While lying in bed in his old Victorian home, a bright light suddenly came straight toward him from his closed and bricked-up fireplace. Then Mike heard these clear and audible words, "You know the way that's right. Walk in it!"

Mike was shocked and immediately sat straight up in bed. God now had his full attention. Then, without hesitation and in the middle of the night, he called his lifeline, Pastor Smith, who conducted his marriage ten years earlier. When the pastor answered the phone, he said, "Scott, I'm lost." That night, the pastor led Mike back to God over the phone." For you see, God never stopped loving Mike or chasing after him. He was always waiting for him with open arms, no matter what he had done.

"...neither death nor life, neither angels nor demons,
neither the present nor the future, nor any powers,
neither height nor depth, nor anything else in all creation,
will be able to separate us from the love of God
that is in Christ Jesus our Lord."
Romans 8:38-39 (NIV)

Mike was a changed person, but he faced a lot of hard work to rebuild his life and recover from many bad decisions. So, the next day, Mike drove an hour to meet with Pastor Smith at his new church. For the next several months, Pastor Smith counseled Mike and helped him rebuild his life following God's word (the Bible). During his counseling

Hope For Your Journey

sessions, Mike finally understood that God did answer his prayers regarding his mother-in-law's illness. He realized she was no longer in pain, fully healed, and in God's heavenly care.

As part of Mike's new journey, he removed hundreds of dollars of "booze" from the top of his refrigerator, then poured the alcohol down his kitchen sink. Mike obediently did this and never regretted it. He also stopped hanging out with his "old partying buddies" to avoid the temptations from his past. Walking away from his buddies was scary; Mike feared he would no longer have friends. Thankfully, God had a plan.

> *"Do not conform to the pattern of this world,*
> *but be transformed by the renewing of your mind.*
> *Then you will be able to test and approve what*
> *God's will is — his good, pleasing and perfect will."*
> *Romans 12:2-3 (NIV)*

Within a short time, Mike met a Mennonite couple through his job. They were loving and compassionate people who volunteered at a local home for quadriplegic people and were looking for a place to stay. So, Mike rented them a room, which helped him spiritually, emotionally, and financially. His new friends invited him to attend their church, and he said yes.

Then, an interesting twist happened. Mike's brother began dating Kate's sister. They soon fell in love and became engaged. In parallel with this news, the pastor of Mike's church started a new speaking series on Sunday mornings called "Marriage, Divorce, and Remarriage." During this time, God revealed to Mike, "I'm not releasing you to date women until you explore every possible opportunity for a marriage reconciliation with Kate." To put it simply, Mike was shocked but listened to God.

> *"My sheep listen to my voice;*
> *I know them, and they follow me."*
> *John 10:27 (NIV)*

On the flip side, Kate was now a strong, independent woman and very different from the person Mike married. She had a steady relationship with another man but did not need "a man" to make her happy. Her career was going well, and their son was happy. Kate was content with her life. She never returned to church after the issues she experienced; involvement with the church was not part of her current life plan.

Rebuilding Your Marriage with God

As wedding plans progressed, Kate was excited to be her sister's maid of honor, and Mike was pleased to be his brother's best man. Due to their roles in the wedding party, they would walk down the aisle together. Kate knew Mike had stopped drinking and renewed his relationship with God – but she had no idea about the marriage reconciliation thoughts God had revealed to him.

In late December 1984, over eleven years after their marriage and four years since their divorce, Mike and Kate began walking down the aisle together at their siblings' wedding with their families watching. Mike suddenly said," Let's walk slowly and smile. I want to shock everyone." Kate went along with Mike's request, and the rumors started to fly among their family and friends.

On January 1, 1985, after reading his morning devotional and striving to be obedient to God, Mike set his New Year's Resolution "To get back together with Kate." About a week later, he prayed, then called Kate and said, "I want to have dinner with you. I want to talk with you." Somewhat reluctantly, she agreed. Once again, Mike faithfully followed God's promptings but was keenly aware that his selfish actions had severely hurt Kate. He knew he did not deserve a second chance with her.

The following week, they met for a nice dinner. During their conversation, Mike said, "Kate, I want to date you; I want to get back together with you." Shocked, Kate burst into laughter, but she could tell he was serious. During the conversation, Mike shared everything God was doing in his life. He was transparent and sincere, so she cautiously listened.

Kate did not know what to think. She didn't trust Mike; part of her heart was still angry with him. In addition, she no longer needed a man in her life, and Mike acquired a lot of debt over the past four years. However, Kate could tell that God was working in his life. She could see the changes. So, she agreed to have another date with him the next day as God began working on her heart.

Over the next several months, they continued to date but endured terrible arguments with each other – they had changed drastically during their four years apart. Then, one day, God revealed to Mike that the issue was not Mike or Kate; their enemy was Satan – he did not want a remarriage to occur.

Hope For Your Journey

With this understanding, they took a leap of faith and went through Christian couples counseling with Pastor Smith. Counseling was an incredible time of healing for both of them. As they talked and prayed together, God began to remold the broken pieces of their relationship. Mike continued to take full responsibility for his actions and was sincerely sorry for the horrible pain he inflicted on Kate.

Counseling was emotional and sometimes overwhelming for Kate as they revisited the pain from past years. However, as the months went by, she began to embrace the true meaning of forgiveness as she humbly sought God's will for her life. Before long, Kate gratefully recommitted her life to God, and He met her with loving, open arms.

"For God so loved the world that he gave his one and only Son,
that whoever believes in him shall not perish but have eternal life."
John 3:16 (NIV)

Somewhere during this painful journey, they fell in love once again. Mike purchased a new ring in the following months and proposed to Kate. Nervously, she said yes as she obediently trusted her Heavenly Father. Then, five years after their divorce, Pastor Smith reunited Mike and Kate in marriage. The past was in the past, thanks to the grace of Jesus. Together, they looked forward to God's plans as a married couple.

"For I know the plans I have for you," declares the Lord,
"plans to prosper you and not to harm you,
plans to give you hope and a future."
Jeremiah 29:11 (NIV)

The first year of marriage was rocky as they adjusted to each other. Satan continued to attack them, but things began to smooth out as they kept trusting God. They prayed together, read their Bibles, and strived to seek God's will for their lives. As a result, their relationship and love for each other grew stronger and stronger.

A few years later, God began preparing Mike's heart to become a minister, but Satan did not want this to happen and attempted to slither back into his thoughts. The adversary started to whisper once again, "You messed up your life so much – God will never use you." Satan also started to chip away at Kate as she questioned how God could use her as a partner in ministry, given their past. But this time, Mike and Kate

Rebuilding Your Marriage with God

turned to God, and He protected them from the enemy. They knew Satan was the master of lies, but God had a specific plan for their lives.

"Put on the full armor of God,
so that you can take your stand
against the devil's schemes."
Ephesians 6:11 (NIV)

With Kate's full support, Mike returned to college and became an ordained minister. During this time, they welcomed a beautiful daughter who completed their family of four. Kate continued to work in the banking industry while serving in various areas of the church. Satan was defeated!

Mike and Kate have now been partners in ministry for nearly forty years. They have a special place in their hearts for couples and individuals struggling in their marriages. God has provided opportunities for them to help hundreds of people who have faltered – and helped them find their way to God. Thankfully, we serve a God of miracles.

"You intended to harm me,
but God intended it for good
to accomplish what is now being done,
the saving of many lives."
Genesis 50:20 (NIV)

In closing, Mike shared, "Kate has been an amazing wife, friend, and incredible partner in ministry. We have been blessed beyond measure – and against all odds. We have personally witnessed that ALL things are possible WITH God. We even had the privilege of watching our son become a minister. No matter what you have done or how you have messed up, there is hope, and His name is Jesus." Then Kate added, "If God can use us, He can use anyone!"

"And we know that in all things God works
for the good of those who love him,
who have been called according to his purpose."
Romans 8:28 (NIV)

Hope For Your Journey

REFLECTION

1. When Mike and Kate's marriage fell apart, people were uncomfortable and failed to reach out to them or offer words of encouragement. Is there someone you know who is hurting or struggling today? How can you reach out and help them?

_____

_____

_____

_____

_____

_____

_____

2. There is power in true forgiveness. Is there someone you need to forgive today?

_____

_____

_____

_____

_____

_____

_____

Rebuilding Your Marriage with God

NEXT STEPS

As we saw in Mike and Kate's story, ALL things are possible with God. Are you struggling with something in your life? Do you need help? Have you messed up?

There is good news! God is available 24/7 to listen to your hurts, anxieties, mistakes, and fears. He will be with you no matter what you have done or what you are facing.

You can pray this simple prayer below:

Dear Heavenly Father,
I need you. Please help me with _____.
Thank you. Amen.

CLOSING PRAYER

Dear Heavenly Father,

Thank you for loving me and never leaving me. Thank you for chasing after me when I mess up and sin. Please help me fulfill your purpose for my life. I love you. Amen.

An Immigrant's Faith

"When I am afraid, I put my trust in you."
Psalm 56:3 (NIV)

In the 1960s, Ginetta (Gina) was born in Genoa, Italy. As the youngest of three children, she grew up in a loving, traditional Italian home. Her father worked on various construction opportunities while her mother cared for their family. They were grateful to qualify for a government-sponsored apartment in a small town outside the city. While Gina's upbringing was modest – love, joy, and amazing food always filled their home.

Their small neighborhood had everything they needed. Like many Italian villages, there were separate stores for the butcher, fresh produce, cheese, and bakery. Gina recalled, "The aroma from the focaccia bread baking on my way to school each morning permeated the air. The smell was incredible."

From an early age, Gina's parents demonstrated the value and importance of a strong work ethic, a lesson she would take into adulthood. Her father worked long hours to ensure their family always had food on the table and a roof over their heads. At the same time, Gina's mother instilled the importance of discipline and responsibility, whether at school or completing home chores. She was strict but ensured her children enjoyed a balanced life, including lots of time to play outside with friends.

"Start children off on the way they should go,
and even when they are old they will not turn from it."
Proverbs 22:6 (NIV)

Gina's parents raised their children to love and honor God. Every Sunday morning, they walked together to their small neighborhood church. Worshiping as a family was a priority – they never missed a Sunday. She shared, "For as long as I can remember, I have believed in God and loved Him."

An Immigrant's Faith

Each summer, Gina's family visited their relatives in Southern Italy. There was always laughter, trips to the beach, and delicious homemade Italian food! While she holds these special vacation memories close to her heart, Gina will never forget a terrifying yet remarkable event that occurred one summer when she was only eight years old.

Gina's family drove to an isolated beach on the beautiful Italian Coast. Her siblings and cousins ran on the beach and played carefree in the sand while their mothers visited. There were no other people on the beach. Then, for some reason, Gina decided to go swimming alone without notifying her mother or any other family member.

At first, Gina enjoyed splashing in the water and jumping over the waves. As she gained additional confidence, she ventured out further into the ocean without a worry in the world. Swimming over and through the waves, Gina was unaware dangerous rip currents were lurking beneath, quickly dragging her out to sea.

When she finally turned around to glance at the shore, Gina was shocked to see how far she had drifted into the ocean and how small the beach looked. Panicked, she immediately started to swim toward the shore. Unfortunately, the harder Gina swam, the further the riptides pulled her out to sea. There was no one else in the water. She was in trouble!

"God is our refuge and strength,
an ever-present help in trouble."
Psalm 46:1 (NIV)

Terrified and exhausted, little Gina knew her life was in danger. She shared, "I was tired and struggling to keep afloat. I thought I was going to die as I had fleeting thoughts of God." Suddenly, out of nowhere, a young man began to swim toward her.

His presence startled her, but she was thankful to no longer be alone. He quietly reached down, removed one of his swimming fins, and told Gina to put it on her foot. He then gave her the second fin. Once the fins were securely on Gina's feet, he pointed to the left and said, "Go that way." He knew she had to swim to the side to get out of the riptide, or she would drown.

"In my distress I called to the Lord;
I cried to my God for help.

From his temple he heard my voice;
my cry came before him, into his ears."
Psalm 18:6 (NIV)

Full of adrenaline, Gina followed his directions. The fins made a big difference as she swam toward the left to escape the powerful under-currents. Despite her exhaustion, once the pressure from the riptides dissipated, Gina swam directly toward the beach. She assumed the man was following her as she finally felt the ground under her feet, then collapsed on the shore, shaking and shivering.

When she turned around to thank the man, he was nowhere to be found. As her eyes darted around the beach and then back to the ocean, she could not locate him anywhere. Gina desperately wanted to return his swimming fins and thank him. She began to panic as fear filled her mind – did he drown? So little Gina began to pray that the man safely swam to another part of the beach.

When Gina finally caught her breath, she ran to her mother and shared the terrifying experience. Together, they looked for the young man without success. When the time came for her family to leave the beach, she left his swimming fins on the sand, hoping he would return to pick them up. To this day, she still prays for him.

Despite her young age, Gina realized God used the young man to save her that day. She shared, "It was a miracle – in my desperation, he suddenly appeared in the ocean, saved my life, and quickly disap-peared with no trace." This event left a profound mark on Gina's heart. It reinforced her faith and provided strength for the future challenges she would face.

"Now faith is confidence in what we hope for
and assurance about what we do not see."
Hebrews 11:1 (NIV)

Time passed quickly, and before long, Gina was in middle school. She was a good student and began to learn French and English. Then, in the blink of an eye, it was time for high school. In Italy, you chose a specific education path for high school called "Scuola Secondaria di Secondo Grado." Gina selected the Technical School for Business. She excelled in her first year of studies and passed with flying colors.

An Immigrant's Faith

Despite her success in school, Gina yearned to do something different. So that summer, at the age of fifteen, she found a job in Genoa and began working as a "shampoo girl" in a small hair salon – the beginning of her future career. Instead of "hanging out" with friends for the summer, Gina chose to catch the early morning bus and work long days standing on her feet. She was not afraid of hard work, was mature for her age, and was very independent.

"Whatever you do, work at it with all your heart,
as working for the Lord..."
Colossians 3:23 (NIV)

As is customary in Italian homes, if you worked outside the home, one-half of your earnings went to your parents to help run the household. Subsequently, her actual earnings were nominal, but she was happy! Gina enjoyed interacting with people from all walks of life and loved using her hands to accomplish work instead of focusing on boring book studies centered around economics and accounting.

As the new school year approached, Gina felt unsettled about her future, so she asked God for guidance. She trusted her Heavenly Father and knew he would clarify her path. Before long, it became clear the traditional neighborhood technical school was not the right path for her. God had a different approach for Gina to fulfill her purpose in life. So, one evening, after days of praying, she bravely approached her strict parents with a surprising proposal.

"Trust in the Lord with all your heart
and lean not on your own understanding;
in all your ways submit to him,
and he will make your paths straight."
Proverbs 3:5-6 (NIV)

Gina's father required his children to graduate with a school certificate to carry them through life – it was non-negotiable. So, she proposed a different path to accomplish her father's requirement while also pursuing her desire to become a licensed hairstylist, which takes five years in Italy. Gina's proposal required an investment from her parents, including tuition to an alternate technical school and an upscale Genoa Hair Academy.

Gina bravely requested that she leave the traditional neighborhood school. Instead, she would continue to live at home and work at the salon in the mornings. In the afternoon, she would attend a specialty business technical school in Genoa and study in the evenings. Upon graduation from technical school, Gina would attend the hair academy while working part-time. Surprisingly, after deep discussions and prayers for guidance, her parents agreed to support her new path. They believed in her.

Thanks to Gina's determination and strong work ethic, she followed the plan. She graduated from technical school and attended the hair academy while working part-time. Then, at the age of eighteen, her boss (Maria) unexpectedly sold the salon and moved to the United States (U.S.) with her son Aldo. Gina quickly landed a job at another salon while completing her hair stylist studies at the academy. She never anticipated her life would later intersect with Maria in a life-altering way.

When she turned nineteen, Gina's life suddenly turned upside down. On a typical Monday morning, she awoke with severe abdominal pain and was unable to stand. Her mother rushed her to the emergency room. The on-call doctor quickly admitted her for several tests to pinpoint the problem, but the tests revealed nothing. Her doctor was perplexed. By late afternoon, she could barely breathe due to the excruciating pain. Gina feared she might die – a sense of desperation she recognized from her near-drowning incident eleven years earlier.

> *"Yea, though I walk through*
> *the valley of the shadow of death,*
> *I will fear no evil: for thou art with me;*
> *thy rod and thy staff they comfort me."*
> *Psalm 23:4 (KJV)*

That evening, after her parents left the hospital, the doctor entered her room with a nurse. He proceeded to say, "I am going to conduct an exploratory surgery so we can figure out what is wrong with you. Independent Gina immediately said, "No, you are not!" The doctor firmly said, "You could die." She replied, "I'll take my chances."

The doctor was extremely agitated as Gina firmly advocated for herself despite the horrific pain. At that point, the doctor looked at the nurse and firmly said, "Monitor her closely. If this girl has a fever or her skin turns yellow, we will bring her into surgery anyway. Continue the IV. Stop all food. She can only have water and tea." With those instructions, he stormed out of the room.

Satan was testing her faith. It appeared Gina was suddenly all alone in the hospital room, facing potential death once again. However, she was not alone. God met her that night in the cold, sterile hospital room as she closed her eyes and prayed harder than ever, "God, please, please don't let this happen. Please save my life!"

"But when you ask, you must believe and not doubt,
because the one who doubts is like a wave of the sea,
blown and tossed by the wind."
James 1:6 (NIV)

As Gina prayed through the night, she felt God's powerful presence fill the room. His love permeated the air as He provided an indescribable sense of peace. As she held tightly to her faith, she could feel fever ravishing throughout her body as the intense pain continued. But Gina chose to keep trusting God. She knew from experience He would never leave her.

Every hour before the nurse appeared to take her temperature, she dragged herself out of bed and staggered to the bathroom sink to splash cold water on her face and chest. Gina did not want the nurse to record a fever as she waited on the Lord for a miracle. As the bathroom light hit her face and body, she noticed her skin was now a jaundiced yellow.

When dawn broke and sunrays filtered into the hospital room, Gina's fever miraculously broke, and her yellowish, jaundiced skin returned to its "normal" color. Her intense pain continued, but she knew God saved her, and she was grateful.

"When I am afraid, I put my trust in you.
In God, whose word I praise —
in God I trust and am not afraid.
What can mere mortals do to me?"
Psalm 56:3-4 (NIV)

Gina shared, "I always believed and trusted God, but that night in the hospital room, I developed a personal relationship with my Heavenly Father that is indescribable. He never left me. I know He performed a miracle. How do I know? – I felt it!"

For an additional five days, the doctor limited her diet to water and tea since they were unable to determine the source of her pain. She was extremely weak. Finally, with no explanation, the pain subsided, and the doctor released her from the hospital with no diagnosis. The pain never returned.

For the next few years, Gina continued to live with her parents, following the tradition of Italian families. Italian women typically did not move from their parents' home until marriage. She began working as a full-time hairstylist at an upscale salon in Genoa and enjoyed her career. She worked long hours but had limited money since half of her income went to her parents.

It was during this time that Gina began to have a recurring dream. She would stand on the ground, look up in the sky, and watch an airplane fly by. The dream perplexed her, and it never changed. For some reason, the dream caused her to reflect on the times God saved her life. She thought, "Why did God save me? Did He have a special plan for her?" With those thoughts, Gina began to pray and ask God to guide and direct the next steps in her life.

> *"For I know the plans I have for you," declares the Lord,*
> *"plans to prosper you and not to harm you,*
> *plans to give you hope and a future."*
> *Jeremiah 29:11 (NIV)*

Then, one day, she received an unexpected letter from Maria, the owner of the first salon where Gina worked as a "shampoo girl." Maria described her amazing life in America and shared that her income was significantly higher compared to Italy. She then extended an opportunity for Gina to work at her salon in Northern Virginia.

At first, she dismissed the job offer. However, as the months passed, Maria sent additional letters stating Gina could live in her basement. She was surprised by Maria's generous offers and assumed good hairstylists must be hard to recruit in America. It never dawned on her that Maria might have other motives, such as marrying her son, Aldo. Gina had previously worked with Aldo at Maria's Italian salon.

The opportunity to work in an American hair salon, make more money, and live away from her parents' home finally piqued Gina's interest. As a hard-working, strong woman, she did not feel fulfilled and desired additional freedom. Perhaps this opportunity was the answer to her current situation. She loved her parents but felt something was missing in her life.

Gina had never traveled beyond the borders of Italy, so the thought of getting on a plane for the first time and traveling to a new country was overwhelming. As the recurring airplane dream continued, she began to envision her life in America. However, fears about living in a foreign country with limited English skills scared her.

So, she once again asked God to guide her, "What should I do, God? Do you want me to stay in Italy with my parents or fly to America and pursue this new opportunity?" Then, she waited on the Lord for an answer.

> *"But they that wait upon the Lord shall renew their strength;*
> *they shall mount up with wings as eagles;*
> *they shall run, and not be weary;*
> *and they shall walk, and not faint."*
> *Isaiah 40:31 (KJV)*

Finally, when Gina was twenty-three, after many conversations with God, she felt He was leading her to pursue the opportunity in the U.S. So, she once again had a serious discussion with her parents. She remembers looking her father in the eye and saying, "Dad, what do you think if I go to the U.S. to expand my career? As you know from Maria's letters, she has a job for me, and I can live in her basement. I know I don't speak English, but I learn quickly."

After many discussions, her father gave his blessings, but her mother had misgivings and was very concerned. In retrospect, Gina shared, "I'm shocked I failed to consider the emotions of my parents, family, and friends as I prepared to fly to a foreign country, not knowing when I would return. I was selfish, focused only on myself – and, as much as I hate to admit it, only prayed for myself. Despite my self-centeredness, God was faithful, and I am grateful."

So, Gina took a leap of faith and did her best to understand the complex U.S. immigration requirements. After obtaining an Italian passport, she went to the U.S. Embassy in Genoa to apply for a visa. After completing numerous forms, providing the required documents, and participating in a detailed interview, Gina received her U.S. visa. Then, trusting God, she purchased a one-way plane ticket to Washington DC, packed one suitcase, said goodbye, and boarded an airplane to pursue a new life in America.

"Have I not commanded you? Be strong and courageous.
Do not be afraid; do not be discouraged,
for the Lord your God will be with you wherever you go."
Joshua 1:9 (NIV)

As Gina settled into Maria's basement and the new job, she was excited to watch her "American Dream" unfold. But her "American Dream" journey was not easy. The language barrier, culture shock, and confusing immigration requirements were frustrating and sometimes overwhelming. Gina proactively advocated for herself whenever possible and asked for help when needed, a skill she acquired many years earlier.

The English she learned in school was far different from American English, so initially, she relied on Maria to translate conversations with customers and co-workers. Thankfully, many Spanish words and phrases were similar to Italian, so she leveraged this communication skill while taking "English as a Second Language" classes during the evenings.

Despite the language barrier, Gina worked extremely hard, and her client base at the salon quickly expanded due to her excellent hair styling skills. She diligently saved money to obtain an immigration attorney to help with the volumes of paperwork required to become a legal U.S. resident. She also paid all the required employment taxes as she positioned herself to eventually become a U.S. citizen – a process that would ultimately take nine years.

Despite the stress, Gina continued to lean on God for His strength and wisdom. Every night before closing her eyes, she thanked God for His blessings and asked for His guidance and peace – a faithful practice she still follows. Gina knew firsthand that with God, all things are possible!

Jesus looked at them and said,
"With man this is impossible,
but with God all things are possible."
Matthew 19:26 (NIV)

Unfortunately, as the weeks passed, Gina realized Maria had significantly changed compared to the woman she knew and worked for in Italy. It was as if her boss had transformed into a person with two diverse personalities. Sometimes, Maria was kind and caring, and on other occasions, she was a cruel, controlling narcissist.

An Immigrant's Faith

Sadly, in the 1980s, people did not openly discuss mental health challenges or know how to help people obtain the proper medical assistance. Subsequently, Gina began to "live on eggshells" 24/7, never knowing which Maria she was dealing with. The stressful situation was exhausting and began to take a toll on Gina's health.

"Do not be anxious about anything, but in every situation,
by prayer and petition, with thanksgiving,
present your requests to God.

And the peace of God, which transcends all understanding,
will guard your hearts and your minds in Christ Jesus."
Philippians 4:6-7 (NIV)

Gina was thankful Maria's son Aldo lived at the house and worked as a hairstylist in his mother's salon. Together, they helped each other survive the ups and downs of Maria's personality. Since Aldo was already a legal U.S. resident and spoke English, he began assisting Gina with her studies. Before long, they became good friends and confided in each other. She was grateful since her family and friends were four-thousand miles away.

Finally, after an exhausting year, Gina and Maria experienced a major "falling out." Gina quit the salon and moved to another basement apartment. She was relieved to be out of the hostile environment and away from Maria – or so she thought.

Due to her excellent hair-styling skills, Gina quickly landed a job at a prestigious hair salon in the famous Watergate Hotel in Washington, DC. It felt great to finally have the freedom she sought while pursuing the American Dream of owning her own business and home. She praised God and thanked Him.

"Give thanks to the Lord, for he is good;
his love endures forever."
Psalm 107:1 (NIV)

As the months passed, Gina and Aldo supported and encouraged each other. As their friendship deepened, they discussed the possibility of co-owning a hair salon. They also, as crazy as it might sound, began to explore a "marriage of convenience." While they were not in love, they deeply cared for each other, shared common goals, and grew up in Italy. Their partnership made sense – well, at least on paper.

A few years later, they married and opened their first hair salon. And yes, Maria became Gina's mother-in-law. Gina finally returned to Italy to see her family and officially became a U.S. resident. Her hopes and dreams were falling into place, but in retrospect, she shared, "While I loved God, prayed daily, and sought His guidance, I was still self-centered and preoccupied with worldly achievements – that would soon change."

After years of waiting, Gina finally met the requirements to apply for a naturalized U.S. citizenship. She had spent nine years learning English (reading, writing, speaking), attending U.S. civics classes, and filling out numerous forms. When the time finally came, Gina passed her naturalization interview and scored 100% on the English and civics tests. She was thrilled.

Gina shared, "I will never forget the day I officially became a U.S. citizen. It was an exciting experience! The government conducted the U.S. Naturalization Oath Ceremony in a historic building located in Washington, D.C. That day, I was the only immigrant from Italy. As our group of immigrants jointly said the oath of allegiance to the United States of America in English, my eyes filled with tears as I quietly thanked God for carrying me through my citizenship journey. He never left me."

> *"The Lord himself goes before you and will be with you;*
> *he will never leave you nor forsake you.*
> *Do not be afraid; do not be discouraged."*
> *Deuteronomy 31:8 (NIV)*

Three years after their marriage, Gina gave birth to a healthy baby boy named Alex. For the first time, she understood what it meant to love someone more than just herself. As their salon business flourished, their marriage of convenience began to falter. However, given their Italian family values, they vowed to hold their marriage together for the sake of their new son. Gina asked God for strength.

> *"Lord, be gracious to us; we long for you.*
> *Be our strength every morning,*
> *our salvation in time of distress."*
> *Isaiah 33:2 (NIV)*

When Alex was three, Gina was once again pregnant. As she entered her seventh month of pregnancy, her world suddenly turned upside down. Alex became extremely ill and was diagnosed with Cystic Fibrosis (CF). There was no cure, and the doctors said his life expectancy would only be nine to thirteen years. She was devastated. In addition, CF was genetic. There was a possibility her unborn child could also have CF and face the same fate.

Gina shared, "I thought it was the end of the world, but thankfully, God once again showed up in my time of need and carried me through a devastating period in my life. Despite my fears, He showed me how to pray for others, not just myself. Through His peace and my hope in Him, I remained strong for the sake of Alex and my unborn baby girl."

She continued, "Thankfully, I knew firsthand God performs miracles despite the human obstacles we may face. So, on my knees, I asked God to heal Alex and to ensure my unborn baby did not have CF. I prayed with the full belief that God would perform miracles for my children."

Eight weeks later, Gina gave birth to a beautiful baby girl named Monica. Thankfully, after several tests, the doctors determined she was a healthy baby and did not have CF. Gina praised God and thanked Him.

> *"Lord, you are my God;*
> *I will exalt you and praise your name,*
> *for in perfect faithfulness*
> *you have done wonderful things..."*
> *Isaiah 25:1 (NIV)*

While little Alex struggled, Gina ensured he received the best medical support available. She shared, "As Alex's health deteriorated, I NEVER lost faith. God faithfully carried me every step of the way. I continued to praise Him while I prayed for a miracle."

Gina continued, "As the months and then years passed, God provided me with an unexplainable sense of peace as Alex began to defy the medical odds. Before long, we celebrated Alex's ninth, thirteenth, twenty-first, and thirty-fifth birthdays. Yes, with God, Alex overcame the doctors' prognoses. While Alex now has minimal issues with CF, God continues to watch over him. He survived a terrifying motorcycle accident in his twenties and overcame lung cancer in his early thirties. Thanks be to God!"

"In the middle of Alex's early struggles, my husband had an affair and walked out, leaving me alone with my children and a struggling salon. Thankfully, God is bigger than any human obstacles the adversary throws at us. By the grace of God, "per grazia di Dio," He picked up the pieces of my life and eventually brought a loving husband and father into our lives. I will forever be grateful."

In closing, Gina said, "During my life, God has faithfully shown up and carried me through my fears, challenges, heartbreaks, and near-death experiences. Thankfully, from the blessings of my children and now my caring husband, I finally understand what it means to love and pray for others. I am certainly not perfect, but God helps me be a better person here on earth, and I will forever be grateful."

> *"Peace I leave with you; my peace I give you.*
> *I do not give to you as the world gives.*
> *Do not let your hearts be troubled and do not be afraid."*
> *John 14:27 (NIV)*

Gina

An Immigrant's Faith

REFLECTION

1. At every turn in Gina's life, she trusted God. Do you recall a time you asked God for His guidance and direction? What happened?

_____

_____

_____

_____

_____

_____

_____

2. Have you ever faced a dangerous or life-altering situation? Did you reach out to God for help, or did you face the problem alone?

_____

_____

_____

_____

_____

_____

Hope For Your Journey

NEXT STEPS

1. Take a moment and do a self-assessment of your priorities and worldly aspirations.

   a. How did you spend your time and energy today? This week? This past month?

   _____

   _____

   _____

   b. How much time did you spend reading the Bible, talking to God, listening to God, or helping others over the last seven days?

   _____

   _____

   _____

2. What is one thing you could change this week to increase your time with God? Some ideas might include attending church, reading the Bible, starting a new devotional, listening to inspirational music, or praying.

CLOSING PRAYER

Dear Heavenly Father,

Thank you for loving me and watching over me, even when I am self-centered and become preoccupied with the ambitions of the world. Please help me keep my focus on you! Amen.

Appearances Can Be Deceiving

"Therefore encourage one another
and build each other up..."
1 Thessalonians 5:11 (NIV)

It was a challenging and stressful year. As the company struggled to meet Wall Street's financial expectations, the leadership team was under tremendous pressure, and a hiring freeze was in place to reduce overhead costs. Nan's business unit faced demanding growth requirements while simultaneously submitting a proposal to win a multi-million-dollar contract.

Nan's team needed additional help, so she formally asked the company to provide a senior growth specialist to pursue the enormous contract. Thankfully, the corporate office agreed but only offered a part-time resource. Nan was grateful for the help, but her challenges were just beginning.

Within a few weeks, Stella started supporting the team from her remote location in Florida. She had an impressive resume, including several $50M+ contract wins, and came highly recommended. Stella continued reporting to her current manager and agreed to fly to the corporate office in Virginia for key business meetings with Nan, as required.

Unfortunately, from the onset, Stella's support was below expectations. She seemed to approach critical assignments with a lackadaisical attitude. Not only did she miss meetings and deadlines, but reports were incomplete, and attention to essential details was lacking. At times, she appeared overwhelmed, and her haphazard approach frustrated Nan and the team.

Nan tried to work with Stella as new concerns surfaced. Finally, Nan reluctantly escalated the concerns to Stella's manager but faced immediate resistance. Her manager and the corporate team were

Hope For Your Journey

confident they had assigned the right person to win this massive contract. Regrettably, Nan had no other resource options. Her hands were tied as Stella's unreliable support continued.

A few months later, the division president scheduled a strategic review for the multi-million-dollar contract pursuit assigned to Nan's business unit. Stella claimed the standard briefing charts were in "good shape" and not to worry. Unfortunately, despite several requests, Stella failed to pre-brief Nan.

Stella was running late the morning of the briefing and showed up to the president's strategic review at the last minute. She looked exhausted, and her clothes were disheveled. After resolving some technical issues, Stella finally started the briefing late and struggled to focus. Her presentation was unpolished and lacked critical pieces of information. Fortunately, Nan and the team stepped in to handle strategic questions from the president. They barely slid through the briefing. It was embarrassing.

Nan was furious and again escalated the performance concerns to Stella's manager. Her manager re-emphasized Stella's impressive track record and implied Nan's expectations were perhaps unreasonable. With no other recourse due to the hiring freeze, Nan contemplated reassigning one of her current employees to lead the strategy for the massive contract. Not an ideal solution, but something had to change.

Fortunately, after the disastrous briefing, Stella's performance significantly improved. It was like a light switch "turned on," and she pushed the restart button. Nan cautiously welcomed Stella's surprising transformation but feared prior behavior and performance concerns would resurface. She carefully monitored Stella's progress, often double-checking decisions and supporting data. The two women tolerated each other and had limited conversations.

Stella once said, "If Nan was talking, most likely I would be rolling my eyes. I didn't care if she was right or wrong. We did not get along and had nothing in common."

As the months passed, Stella performed her assignment with excellence. She won the huge contract for Nan's organization and the company. They were both grateful when the project ended but made no attempt to "mend fences" and chose to go their separate ways.

Appearances Can Be Deceiving

Sadly, Nan never asked Stella if she was OK or paused to think something in her life might be causing the performance challenges. Despite being a Christian, Nan never prayed for her or attempted to rebuild a positive relationship. Conversely, she made judgments about Stella, never realizing Stella was in survival mode and suffering in silence.

"Carry each other's burdens,
and in this way you will fulfill the law of Christ."
Galatians 6:2 (NIV)

However, things are not always as they appear. In fact, appearances can be deceiving. Nan's "powerful business façade" at the office was quite different at home. She was a loving mother, daughter, friend, and an abused wife. She lived on eggshells at home, never knowing when her tyrant husband would explode into another rampage.

Nan suffered quietly for years without reaching out for help. It was a painful and lonely existence. It took every ounce of energy in her body to fulfill requirements at work while striving to keep peace at home. Like Stella, she was also in survival mode and suffering in silence.

Thankfully, through a series of miracles, God rescued Nan from a tormented marriage. She was grateful. Her new lease on life soon opened an unexpected chapter – Nan became a Christian author. Never in her wildest dreams did she anticipate this new chapter in her life would include Stella!

After a successful first book, Nan sought God's direction regarding who to interview for her next book of inspirational short stories. Then, one day, a LinkedIn article from Stella "popped up." Nan thought it was odd. She never noticed posts from Stella, and they had not talked or interacted online for over three years.

Nan glanced at the article and was surprised it focused on overcoming drug addiction. Suddenly, God whispered to Nan, "Call Stella. She has a story for you." The unmistakable fatherly voice shocked Nan and "stopped her in her tracks." She immediately paused and thought, "God wants me to reach out to Stella. I don't want to reach out to Stella. We don't even get along." That evening, Nan chose to ignore God's prompting.

A few days later, a second post from Stella popped up about overcoming a drug addiction. Nan thought, "OK, this is weird. Why am I

Hope For Your Journey

suddenly seeing posts from Stella." Once again, God whispered to Nan and reminded her, "Call Stella. She has a story for you." This time, God had her attention – this was not a coincidence!

"My sheep listen to my voice;
I know them, and they follow me."
John 10:27 (NIV)

The adversary immediately placed doubts in Nan's head regarding God's direction, "What will Stella think if you call her? Will she think you're crazy? Will she even talk to you?" Then, it dawned on her, "Wait. God is with me. He is directing me to call Stella. Stop fretting"

"For I am the Lord your God
who takes hold of your right hand
and says to you, Do not fear; I will help you."
Isaiah 41:13 (NIV)

Striving to be obedient and not allowing procrastination to take control, Nan prayed and asked God to be with her as she prepared to call Stella. With some hesitation, and despite her pride and lingering fears, Nan took a deep breath, picked up the cell phone, and pressed the call button.

The phone rang once, twice, then three times before she heard Stella's voice prompting her to leave a message. Nan was quietly relieved when Stella did not answer her phone. However, to be obedient to God's promptings, she left a voice message stating she was writing a second book and looking for inspirational stories. Nan mentioned Stella's posts on LinkedIn and said she wanted to talk.

Nan did not stop there. She sent Stella a short, private message on LinkedIn, "Hi. I just left you a phone message." She also provided her phone number and information about her first book. The situation was now in God's hands, and Nan was relieved.

Thirty minutes later, Stella responded to Nan's LinkedIn message, "Can't wait to get your book. I have quite a story and would love to share it with you. Give me a ring, and let's catch up."

Nan immediately picked up the phone and called Stella. The conversation that followed was nothing short of a miracle. God bonded the two women in a unique and powerful way. Nan learned Stella was a single

Mom, and while they were working together, her teenage son became addicted to heroin. She was in and out of the office as she tried to save his life and keep him out of jail. But there was so much more...

As their open and enlightening discussion continued, Nan bravely revealed the domestic abuse she endured when they were working together. Stella was shocked. She assumed Nan never faced adversity, never had a hair out of place, and enjoyed a simple but superficial life. Both women apologized for the assumptions and judgments they made about each other. The conversation was healing and therapeutic.

> *"The light shines in the darkness,*
> *and the darkness has not overcome it."*
> *John 1:5 (NIV)*

A few weeks later, Nan interviewed Stella for the upcoming book. As they talked, Nan heard the horrific events that occurred before Stella's presentation to the company president. In the middle of the night, while alone in a hotel room, Stella received a panicked phone call from her son's roommate in Colorado. Her son, Alex, had overdosed on heroin, was not breathing, and had been rushed to the hospital. No further information was available.

Stella spent several agonizing hours on the phone, dealing with the hospital and police department, as she desperately tried to find out if Alex was dead or alive. Sadly, they were not helpful. Finally, when the police "booking report "was available online at 8 AM ET, Stella learned Alex was alive and under arrest for drug possession.

Grateful that Alex was still alive, Stella pulled herself together, drove to the office, presented the briefing, and tried to handle questions. She never divulged her horrific night or the fears bombarding her mind. After a long, exhausting day, she quietly returned to her hotel room.

That evening, Stella, who was raised in an atheist home, got down on her hands and knees and started to pray to God for the first time. Sobbing, she said, "God, I don't know who you are. I don't even know if you are real, but I need you to save my son." Our Heavenly Father immediately met her right where she was – in the solitude of a hotel room.

> *"Hear my prayer, Lord, listen to my cry for help;*
> *do not be deaf to my weeping..."*
> *Psalm 39:12 (NIV)*

Hope For Your Journey

From that moment on, Stella "let go" of her anxieties and fears – and turned them over to God. Like a light switch, her life began to improve. She had peace in her mind and heart for the first time in months, thanks to her willingness to fully trust God with her son's life.

For Nan, the perplexing pieces of the puzzle about Stella finally came together. The information regarding the night before and after the strategic briefing took her breath away. She praised God for coming to Stella's rescue. It was a miracle.

Stella continues to embrace and follow God. Her remarkable story has touched hundreds of lives through speaking engagements and social media posts. Stella's son, Alex, is living proof that God performs miracles. He is enjoying a productive life, free from the bondage of drug addiction.

God is in the business of restoration and forgiveness! A few months after the book interview, Nan had the opportunity to recommend Stella for a new consulting job – a position she performed with excellence. Their relationship finally came full circle. They were grateful.

Stella recently told a friend, "Nan is one of my favorite people." The two women share a special bond for life. With God, ALL things are possible!

Appearances Can Be Deceiving

REFLECTION

Appearances can be deceiving.

Have you ever made wrong assumptions and judgments about a person or situation?

What happened? How did you feel?

Hope For Your Journey

NEXT STEPS

Take a moment and be honest with yourself.

Do you make assumptions about people or situations? Do you judge people? Do you want God to help you change your feelings and behaviors?

God is available 24/7. You can pray this simple prayer.

Dear Heavenly Father,
I have a habit of making assumptions and judging people. Please help me stop this habit and replace this behavior with positive acts of kindness. I want my thoughts and actions to be pleasing to you. Thank you. Amen.

CLOSING PRAYER

Dear Heavenly Father,

Appearances can be deceiving. Please help me to love people instead of judging them or making assumptions. Thank you for forgiving me for my mistakes and bad decisions. Thank you for restoring relationships. I love you. Amen.

Overcoming An Opioid Dependency

"I can do all things through Christ who strengthens me."
Philippians 4:13 (NKJV)

Excruciating and chronic pain overwhelmed Julie's body and consumed her thoughts — the simple act of standing up sent gut-wrenching pain up and down her spine. As tears rolled down her face, she once again reached for pain pills and muscle relaxers. Slowly, she put the prescription drugs in her mouth, took a few gulps of cold water, and cried out to God for help.

Julie grew up in a small town but moved to Southern California to escape her past. After surviving a tough childhood, rebellious teenage years, and a wild ride in her twenties, she finally settled down when she met and married Steve. He had a positive and stabilizing impact on Julie's tumultuous life. They were happy.

In her mid-thirties, Julie began to experience flashbacks from her childhood and realized she needed help. Thankfully, when she was a little girl, her grandmother taught her about the love and power of God. Then, one day, during a horrific flashback, Julie remembered the stories about God and cried out to Him for help. He immediately met her right where she was and surrounded her with loving friends and family.

"The Lord is close to the brokenhearted
and saves those who are crushed in spirit."
Psalm 34:18 (NIV)

Julie's Christian friends and neighbors began to pray for her and extended invitations to attend church events. These simple acts of love changed her life. Slowly, Julie began to deepen her relationship with God by reading the Bible, attending Bible studies, and finally accepting Jesus as her personal savior.

During this healing journey, God restored Julie's emotional life, giving her peace, hope, and the ability to forgive others. She was grateful. Yet, she had no idea how her strong faith and relationship with God would soon become "a lifeline" as unforeseen challenges again entered her life.

*"We who have run for our very lives to God
have every reason to grab the
promised hope with both hands and never let go.
It's an unbreakable spiritual lifeline,
reaching past all appearances
right to the very presence of God ..."*
Hebrews 6:19-20 (MSG)

When Julie was thirty-eight, life was finally going well, with only an occasional bump in the road. She had a promising career as a computer operator, including a competitive salary with excellent benefits. Steve and Julie had a beautiful home and exciting plans for their future. However, we live in a fallen world. Sometimes, bad things happen to good people.

It was a typical day at the office, but it changed Julie's life forever. Her job required constant motion, including walking, reaching, and lifting. But on this day, the simple act of standing up from a chair took Julie to her knees and brought tears to her eyes. The pain in her back was excruciating. She was unable to catch her breath, sit, or stand. What happened?

As Julie desperately prayed for relief, the doctors determined she had torn a disc in her back, which caused her spinal cord to lose fluid. It was a severe injury. For the next six months, she was unable to work.

Thankfully, Julie's employer proactively set up Workman's Compensation income as she suffered 24/7 from the excruciating pain in her back. She could not stand, sit, or sleep without taking the legally prescribed pain pills and muscle relaxers. Sadly, Julie's body became dependent on opioid pain medication. She did not fully comprehend what this meant or the future implications she would soon face.

When Julie's Workman Compensation disability checks ended, she was still in agony and could not perform the functions of a computer operator or any other position. They desperately needed additional income to pay their bills. Julie was emotionally and physically exhausted.

> *"Come to me, all you who are weary*
> *and burdened, and I will give you rest."*
> *Matthew 11:28 (NIV)*

During a conversation with her employer, they suggested she apply for Social Security Disability Insurance due to her severe back injury. Julie had no idea how to apply for this insurance but desperately needed income to offset their financial obligations. So, she completed the required paperwork, despite the brain fog from her medication, and asked God to take care of the situation.

About six weeks later, she received a rejection letter from the Social Security Administration, denying her request for disability support. Julie did not know what to do, and she sobbed. Over the next few days, she prayed for God's guidance, then waited on the Lord as her debilitating pain continued.

> *"...but those who hope in the Lord*
> *will renew their strength.*
> *They will soar on wings like eagles;*
> *they will run and not grow weary,*
> *they will walk and not be faint."*
> *Isaiah 40:31 (NIV)*

Then, a miracle happened. Out of the blue, Julie received a second letter from the Social Security Administration, not only approving her disability insurance but also providing a $10,000 check to cover the weeks when she did not receive disability payments. Julie burst into tears as she praised God.

> *"For with God nothing shall be impossible."*
> *Luke 1:37 (KJV)*

A month later, Julie had back surgery to finally fix her torn disc. The doctor inserted metal between two vertebrae, but he placed the metal between the wrong vertebrae due to his misdiagnosis. After the surgery, her back pain intensified, and the doctor was perplexed. After several follow-up appointments, Julie's doctor referred her to a pain management clinic, never realizing he had made a surgical mistake.

The appointments at the pain clinic were humiliating, and she sometimes felt like a criminal. To schedule the initial doctor visit, she was required to pass a mandatory drug test and complete a lengthy questionnaire regarding her past drug use, both prescribed and not prescribed. She also had to agree to participate in future random drug testing.

Julie was required to bring her prescription drug bottles to each appointment. It was degrading to watch the nurses count the remaining pills in her bottles to ensure she was not abusing the medications. Julie was continually puzzled by the clinic's embarrassing activities since she never abused her prescriptions or took illegal drugs for her back pain.

As Julie's nightmare continued, the pain clinic increased her daily opioid (OxyContin) dosage to reduce her suffering. The highly addictive drug caused severe headaches, fatigue, increased brain fog, loss of appetite, and stomach pain. She was caught in a vicious cycle of pain and side effects and did not know how to escape. Julie later discovered the pain clinic endangered her life by subscribing dangerous levels of OxyContin (240mg daily).

Thankfully, Julie obtained a referral to a different outpatient pain management center. At this new clinic, she learned her body's dependency on OxyContin was an addiction (now called an opioid use disorder.) Julie was shocked and mortified as she thought, "How did this happen? I carefully took my legally prescribed medications to relieve my debilitating pain. Now I'm addicted to this medication and still have pain?"

The new clinic immediately placed Julie on a detox protocol to slowly reduce her pain medication, which unfortunately increased her pain. Julie feared she might suffer from chronic pain 24/7 for the rest of her life. She once again cried out to God for help.

"The Lord is my rock, my fortress, and my deliverer;
my God is my rock, in whom I take refuge,
my shield and the horn of my salvation, my stronghold."
Psalm 18:2 (NIV)

Julie shared, "Due to my horrific pain, I could not accomplish many simple tasks people take for granted. The mere act of sitting on a toilet or putting on clothes was gut-wrenching. Then, in the middle of my storm, Satan began to whisper defeating thoughts in my head, causing self-doubt, guilt, and worthlessness. Thankfully, I knew I was a daughter of God, and HE LOVED ME. Therefore, I chose to hold on to God's promises as my pain journey continued. I knew God would eventually heal me, either here on earth or in heaven."

"Heal me, Lord, and I will be healed;
save me, and I will be saved,
for you are the one I praise."
Jeremiah 17:14 (NIV)

Julie found an outstanding doctor who performed a second back surgery the following year. As a result, Julie's pain immediately subsided. As time passed, she was only half a pill away (per day) from being totally off her opioid prescription. Unfortunately, as her back continued to heal, she was in a car accident. Sadly, her back was re-injured, and the vicious pain cycle started again.

At first, the increased dosage of OxyContin controlled Julie's pain from the car accident, and she was grateful. Then, breakthrough pain began to occur, so the doctor increased her dosages to alarming levels as they tried to reduce her suffering. Julie was again dependent on opioids while living with chronic pain.

Julie's long-term pain nightmare also included other prescription drugs such as muscle relaxers, Trazadone (to sleep), and the highly addictive Xanax to help reduce her anxiety.

She shared, "Chronic pain and the dependence on prescribed medications is a hard way to live. It's physically and emotionally draining – the pain <u>NEVER</u> stops. You have NO peace. Sadly, on many days, I became a prisoner in my own home, living on the couch or in bed with my heating pad. I missed many family gatherings and outings with friends. It made me sad."

She continued, "To make the situation worse – people, including family members, stereotyped me, whispered behind my back, and cast judgment about my prescription dependency. Bottom line, I sought professional medical help for my painful back injuries and ended up with an unexpected and unwanted drug dependency. I never went to a dark street corner to make a drug deal. Living with chronic pain is horrific, but the painful judgment of others was demoralizing. Thankfully, God knows the truth and my story!"

"Do not judge, or you too will be judged.
For in the same way you judge others,
you will be judged, and with the measure you use,
it will be measured to you."
Matthew 7:1-2 (NIV)

Hope For Your Journey

As Julie's health battle continued, her husband's job required a move to a beautiful remote mountain community. She quickly found a new pain management clinic as she continued her dependence on opioids and other prescriptions. Despite the gorgeous forest and wildlife surrounding their new home, her world kept shrinking as she lived from pill to pill, trying to survive the relentless 24/7 back pain.

Julie continued reporting to the pain clinic every month, which was a requirement to get her prescriptions. Medications were limited to a 30-day supply, with no exceptions. Therefore, Julie's on-time refills were critical since she did not "stash away" pills for "tough days" or potential emergencies.

When Julie turned fifty, an unprecedented storm hit the Rocky Mountains just one day before her 30-day prescription pick-up. The storm dumped over twelve inches of rain within thirty-six hours, resulting in a catastrophic 100-year flood. Julie and Steve's home had no electricity or drinkable water, and their basement had six feet of dirty, standing water. The floods demolished the only highway out of their community and wiped out numerous country roads. They were trapped.

The U.S. President declared a state of emergency for the entire region to help evacuate thousands of stranded people. The raging waters destroyed many homes and businesses in their local community. Grocery stores, medical facilities, pharmacies, and her pain management clinic were flooded or unreachable.

Listening to handheld ham radios, they learned helicopter evacuations were underway by the Army and National Guard. They hoped to conduct mandatory evacuations in their community within four days.

The reality and severity of Julie's opioid dependency became crystal clear. She only had one OxyContin and one sleeping pill remaining. She was facing increased pain and potential drug withdrawals.

As Julie begged God for His help and intervention, she carefully cut the remaining pills into quarters to extend her medication. She also kept a journal to ration the pills. Thankfully, God heard her cries. Due to adrenaline rushes and flood distractions, she survived her excruciating back pain and thankfully experienced no withdrawal symptoms. It was a miracle. Julie was grateful and praised God!

"Lord, hear my prayer, listen to my cry for mercy;
in your faithfulness and righteousness
come to my relief."
Psalm 143:1 (NIV)

When Day 4 finally arrived, she took a small backpack and suitcase to the local fire department, boarded an Army helicopter, and evacuated to Fort Collins. As they took off, her eyes filled with tears as they flew over miles of devastation. It was gut-wrenching. Steve stayed behind for twenty-four hours to remove the remaining water from their basement and disinfect the flooded areas in their home.

When the helicopter landed in Fort Collins, Julie's brother met her and immediately took her to the local pharmacy. As she got in the car and opened the bag of pills, God whispered, "What are your current pain levels? Do you need to take the recommended full dosage?" It was a powerful "ah-ha" moment.

When Steve evacuated the following day, he joined Julie at her brother's home. Their mandatory evacuation lasted six long weeks. During this time, Julie began a major soul-searching journey with God. She spent hours talking with her Heavenly Father. At one point, she cried out to the Lord, "I do not want to depend on anything but you. Please help me."

"Heal me, Lord and I will be healed;
save me and I will be saved,
for you are the one I praise."
Jeremiah 17:14 (NIV)

During their six-week evacuation, Julie carefully paid attention to her pain levels and slowly reduced her opioid dosages without medical intervention or withdrawals. She was grateful. Yet, despite her progress, her body still demanded large opioid dosages to reduce her 24/7 pain.

A week after they returned home, Julie stopped taking all her drugs without medical intervention, unaware this decision could have caused seizures, a heart attack, or even death. Julie lived through hell for four long days as her body suffered violent opioid and drug withdrawals.

The pain throughout her body was excruciating as she desperately craved the addictive medications – her vomiting was violent as she lay on the bathroom floor. Julie's non-stop dreams were dark, scary, and psychotic. It was as if she was in a spiritual battle for her heart and soul. At some points, when Julie was too weak to pray, she would quietly say, "Jesus."

Satan continually challenged her, whispering, "Just take the pills!" But thankfully, God gave her the strength to fight and not fall backward. Finally, after four horrific days, Julie was free. She was off all her meds, except Tylenol, to help curb her back pain.

She shared, "The Lord heard my cries and set me free. I still had horrible back pain, but my brain fogginess and other side effects were gone. I was SO grateful."

"The righteous cry out, and the Lord hears them;
He delivers them from all their troubles."
Psalm 34:17 (NIV)

The doctors at the pain clinic were shocked when Julie revealed she was off all her meds. They quickly educated her on the extreme risk she took with her life but were also happy for her newly found freedom. The staff continued to monitor her progress and pain levels over the following weeks.

Unfortunately, her freedom from opioids and other medications was short-lived. Two months later, Julie re-injured her back. Once again, the pain was excruciating, and she could not function.

Immediately, Satan began to whisper, "It's okay, Julie. Just take one pill for this pain. Nothing bad will happen." Due to her unbearable back pain, she swallowed just one OxyContin pill, then two, and within 48 hours, she was hooked again. She felt defeated.

"Be alert and of sober mind.
Your enemy the devil prowls around like a roaring lion
looking for someone to devour."
1 Peter 5:8 (NIV)

When Julie returned to the pain clinic, the "stash" meds she had accumulated over the past few months were gone. Pain signals were bombarding her brain, and she was exhausted. As the doctors tried to counteract her severe pain, they prescribed the highest legal limit of

Overcoming An Opioid Dependency

opioid medications allowed, along with sleeping, anxiety, and muscle relaxer pills. She was a prisoner to drugs once again.

Over the next four years, doctors tried different opioids and approaches, but sadly, breakthrough pain levels would flatten Julie. Nothing seemed to work. One pain clinic forced her to take steroid shots in her back along with pain patches and the opioid Percocet. Her pain only intensified. She finally refused additional treatments.

> *"I have the right to do anything," you say—*
> *but not everything is beneficial.*
> *"I have the right to do anything"—*
> *but not everything is constructive.*
> *1 Corinthians 10:23 (NIV)*

Julie was tired of her pain and ineffective "ball and chain" medications. So, she once again turned to God. But this time, her cousin Mary joined her in prayer to release Julie's pain and opioid dependency to the Lord. They asked God to heal her back and obliterate her drug dependencies. As they prayed, Julie felt her pain beginning to ease. It was amazing!

She shared, "I prayed for years that God would heal me – here on earth or in heaven. But something was different this time in my journey. I finally realized that God created me. Only He knew what I needed and when I needed it."

Julie immediately cut all her medications in half because she knew God had healed her. Then, walking in faith, she bravely stopped all her medications. However, this time, a miracle occurred. She had no drug withdrawals, and her back pain continued to diminish. As she trusted and praised God, her cravings for the medications subsided. She had her life back. Praise God!

> *Jesus looked at them and said,*
> *"With man this is impossible,*
> *but with God all things are possible."*
> *Matthew 19:26 (NIV)*

"I fully trusted God with ALL my life, including my excruciating pain and embarrassing addiction. I gave it ALL to Him. But this time, I also believed He had already healed me. I completely relied on His promises in my human weakness. Thankfully, He met me right where I was and never let go!"

Hope For Your Journey

> *"But when you ask, you must believe and not doubt,*
> *because the one who doubts is like a wave of the sea,*
> *blown and tossed by the wind."*
> *James 1:6 (NIV)*

Six years have now passed. Julie still has back pain, but Tylenol and her favorite heating pad easily control it. When Satan tries to whisper in her ear, she sends him directly to Jesus. It is no longer her battle. God has her in the palm of His hand!

She said, "I am grateful for all the doctors who strived to help me. Sadly, the science and medical breakthroughs that God meant for good, Satan turned into a weapon that haunts and controls millions of people."

> *"Put on the full armor of God,*
> *so that you can take your stand against*
> *the devil's schemes."*
> *Ephesians 6:11 (NIV)*

In closing, Julie said, "Do I believe in miracles? YES! Just look at my life. Praise God!"

WARNING: If you have a dependency on opioids or other medications, ALWAYS seek the advice of your doctor BEFORE stopping your medications.

Overcoming An Opioid Dependency

REFLECTION

1. Do you know someone struggling with an opioid or other drug dependency?

   - Are you praying for them?

   - Are you trying to help them?

   - Are you judging them?

2. Living with pain (physical or emotional) is exhausting. What types of pain have you dealt with in your life? Have you asked God to help you?

_____

_____

_____

_____

_____

_____

_____

_____

_____

_____

_____

_____

Hope For Your Journey

NEXT STEPS

1. Do you have an opioid or other drug dependency? Are you suffering in silence, or do you want to seek help?

   Below are some resources if you want to take the next step:

   - https://www.samhsa.gov/find-help/national-helpline
   - SAMHSA's National Helpline: <u>1-800-662-HELP (4357)</u>

CLOSING PRAYER

Dear Heavenly Father,

Please give me compassion to see all people as your children. Please be with the millions of people who are struggling with chronic pain and opioid dependencies. Remind me to pray for people suffering from addictions. Help me stop judging people.

Thank you! Amen.

The Freedom Honor Flight

"Be devoted to one another in love.
Honor one another above yourselves."
Romans 12:10 (NIV)

It was an ordinary August morning on the outskirts of Washington, DC. Dan arrived at Dulles Airport two hours before his flight, planning to get some work done. On his way to the security checkpoint, he noticed a large crowd. Curious to see what was happening, he walked closer and observed people carrying American flags and signs that read, "Thank you for your service."

A woman dressed in bright yellow was energetically speaking to the crowd. Then she announced, "The flight landed, and our veterans will soon arrive in the airport lobby." The crowd cheered as Dan realized he was in the middle of a welcome celebration for a Freedom Honor Flight. This heartfelt program makes it possible for elderly and terminally ill WWII, Korean War, and Vietnam veterans to visit Washington, DC, and finally see the memorials that stand in their honor.

The crowd quickly swelled to over three hundred people from all walks of life. Dan glanced at his watch and decided he wanted to be part of this special celebration – this was a once-in-a-lifetime opportunity. So, he joined in as strangers politely lined up on both sides of a long walkway to form a "human tunnel of appreciation and gratitude" for the war heroes. The excitement grew as the crowd eagerly anticipated the veterans' arrival.

Finally, the doors from the airport's secure area opened, and the crowd went wild. Americans, young and old, waved flags, held up signs, and cheered. A few moments later, the elderly veterans began to emerge. Some were in wheelchairs, others walked with canes, and a few carefully walked with assistance. Through the cheers, you could hear heartfelt shouts of "Thank you for your service" from the crowd.

"Therefore encourage one another and build each other up..."
1 Thessalonians 5:11 (NIV)

As one man slowly walked through the "tunnel of appreciation," his eyes brimmed with tears. Then he stopped, looked around, and simply said, "WOW." Some veterans paused to shake hands with their new friends in the crowd while others passed by, overwhelmed with gratitude.

As the progression of veterans continued to unfold, time seemed to stand still. Nothing else mattered as people celebrated with love, smiles, and gratitude. Strangers took time from their busy schedules, political disagreements, and pressures of life to express their sincere appreciation for our aging veterans. These veterans made significant sacrifices to ensure we have the right to worship and honor God without retribution.

Dan cheered as tears swelled in his eyes – the joy and emotion of the event touched his heart. Then he thought, "What would the world look like if people from all walks of life would simply love and support each other every day, not just for special occasions? What if people followed Jesus's commandment to love one another?"

"A new command I give you: Love one another.
As I have loved you, so you must love one another."
John 13:34 (NIV)

Finally, the last veterans came through the tunnel on their way to the tour bus. The crowd slowly dispersed, with people going their separate ways. But for a moment, love and gratitude united a group of strangers – perhaps it was a glimpse of Heaven.

The Freedom Honor Flight

REFLECTION

1. When was the last time you unconditionally demonstrated gratitude and appreciation to someone in your life? What did you do to give them hope for their journey? How did you feel? How did your actions impact that person?

_____

_____

_____

_____

_____

_____

_____

2. When was the last time you showed love and compassion to a stranger? What did you do to give them hope for their journey? How did it feel? How did your actions impact that person?

_____

_____

_____

_____

_____

_____

_____

Hope For Your Journey

NEXT STEPS

We are ALL children of God, and He loves us. Unfortunately, we tend to avoid <u>personally</u> interacting with strangers or people who are "not like us." We may donate to important causes, but we tend not to engage personally.

What is one way you can <u>personally</u> engage to help a stranger this week?

> Some ideas might include donating your time to a food kitchen, picking up an elderly person for a church function, delivering meals on wheels, or smiling and saying "hello" to someone you do not know.

CLOSING PRAYER

Dear Heavenly Father,

Help me fulfill your commandment to "Love one another." Amen.

Choosing Faith Over Fear

"Trust in the Lord with all your heart
and lean not on your own understanding;
in all your ways submit to him,
and he will make your paths straight."
Proverbs 3:5-6 (NIV)

Matt and Laura were best friends and fell in love. After college graduation, they married and began to live the "American Dream" in Northern Virginia. They had great jobs and were striving to save money to purchase their first home. They were involved in their local church and enjoyed many activities with close friends and extended family. Life was terrific, and they were excited about their future!

Matt graduated with a degree in sports management and had specific career aspirations. But God had different plans. Shortly after their marriage, the Lord began whispering to Matt and tugging on his heart. It quickly became apparent God was calling him into ministry.

Striving to obey God's calling, Laura and Matt faithfully prayed together as they sought their Heavenly Father's will for their lives. Before long, with Laura's full support, Matt accepted the Youth Minister position at their local church. They had no idea this initial step would be the beginning of an incredible, faith-filled journey.

Matt served alongside a visionary lead pastor and mentor named James Heyward. Pastor James strived to reach outside the church walls and seek "hurting people" in their local community. He mentored Matt and members of the church on the importance of helping the homeless, children in foster care, and victims of sex trafficking. He encouraged people to "get out of their comfort zones" and fulfill God's plan for the church and their lives.

"Therefore go and make disciples of all nations, baptizing them
in the name of the Father and of the Son and of the Holy Spirit,

and teaching them to obey everything I have commanded you.
And surely I am with you always, to the very end of the age."
Matthew 28:19-20 (NIV)

Matt enjoyed being a Youth Pastor and occasionally had the opportunity to preach on Sunday mornings. He was a gifted speaker, and it was evident God had great plans for him. Striving to obey the Lord's calling into the ministry field, Matt started the required college classes to become an ordained pastor. He attended online courses at night and on the weekends. Then, one day, out of the blue, Pastor James said, "I believe you will be the next pastor of our church."

Matt was surprised and somewhat shocked by Pastor James' comment. He had no idea his words would eventually become a reality – but only after he and Laura completed an unexpected, faith-filled journey with God. This journey would be full of miracles and unforgettable events saturated with eye-opening, gut-wrenching, and growth experiences.

A year after they were married, Matt and Laura purchased a 2300-square-foot townhome at a bargain price. A few years later, they welcomed their first daughter, Camden, into the world. Laura left her full-time position as a special education teacher to accept a part-time office manager role at their church. The flexible position allowed her to spend additional time with their daughter. Despite the significant pay cut, God took care of their finances, and they were thankful. Life was great, and they were comfortable.

As the months passed, God began whispering to Matt once again, but this time, the whispers centered around starting new churches. Laura and Matt discussed the situation and prayed for clarity as they strived to obey their Heavenly Father despite their initial feelings and concerns. They were surprised at the timing and direction of God's whispers and a little frustrated since things were going smoothly in their lives.

"Many are the plans in a person's heart,
but it is the Lord's purpose that prevails."
Proverbs 19:21 (NIV)

Matt shared, "We were comfortable in our current ministry assignment and wrestled with this new calling, so we asked God, "Are you sure you want us to leave our current jobs, our new home, and go plant (start) churches with our new baby?" We quickly learned that the miracles God wants to perform in our lives – lie just on the other side of comfort. God was waiting for us to trust Him."

> *"Trust in the Lord with all your heart*
> *and lean not on your own understanding;*
> *in all your ways submit to him,*
> *and he will make your paths straight."*
> *Proverbs 3:5-6 (NIV)*

Despite their comfortable situation and human desires, Matt and Laura continued to pray for guidance. With open minds and trusting hearts, they faithfully sought God's will and direction regarding their next steps. Deep down, they both knew God's timing is always perfect. They wanted to be obedient and fulfill their Heavenly Father's purpose for their lives.

That Thanksgiving, they were driving to the Midwest to celebrate the holiday with Matt's parents, a trip they had made many times before. They were using their GPS to monitor the traffic and projected arrival time. Then, for no apparent reason, their GPS guided them on a new, unfamiliar route. Suddenly, they were overlooking the skyline of Chicago. Simultaneously, they looked at each other and said, "This is it!" They immediately knew God was calling them to Chicago.

Then, through another "God Instance" (because there are no coincidences), Matt and Laura attended a wedding and connected with a couple who were planting (starting) a new church in Chicago. They knew God's fingerprints were all over this "chance meeting" and continued to pray for their Heavenly Father's direction as doors began to open. While His plan for their next steps continued to unfold, they were still unclear about how, when, and where they should start their ministry.

> *"The Lord himself goes before you and will be with you;*
> *he will never leave you nor forsake you.*
> *Do not be afraid; do not be discouraged."*
> *Deuteronomy 31:8 (NIV)*

The following months flew by as God began to "fill in the blanks" regarding their upcoming ministry. As He continued to open new doors, it became apparent they would support and minister to people living in the Lakeview neighborhood, which was part of the inner city

Hope For Your Journey

of Chicago. Their goal was to "love your neighbor as yourself" (Mark 12:31), meet people right where they were without judging, and lovingly share the hope of Jesus through word and deeds.

Whether people were struggling physically, mentally, emotionally, financially, or spiritually – regardless of their backgrounds or beliefs – Matt and Laura would strive to be the hands and feet of Jesus. They would live downtown so they could readily minister and help people 24/7, including the homeless, victims of sex and labor trafficking, prostitutes, neighbors, marginalized members of the LGBTQ+ community, single moms, refugees, victims of domestic abuse, runaways, and drug addicts. God gave them a vast mission field and said, "GO!"

At times, this new path seemed unreasonable and impossible. The thought of selling their townhome and furniture, moving to an unfamiliar area, having no job prospects with hovering college debt, nurturing a baby in a high crime area, and leaving their support group of friends and family was overwhelming. Despite the uncertainties, they kept seeking God's direction while asking Him to silence the lies and negative whispers from the enemy (Satan).

Then, one day. God brought a Bible verse (John 6:16-21) alive for them during a morning devotion. This new path and ministry would be impossible if they did not "invite Jesus into the boat" to lead their way, give them wisdom, and provide protection.

"When evening came,
his disciples went down to the lake,
where they got into a boat
and set off across the lake for Capernaum.
By now it was dark, and Jesus had not yet joined them.
A strong wind was blowing and the waters grew rough.
When they had rowed about three or four miles,
they saw Jesus approaching the boat,
walking on the water; and they were frightened.
But he said to them, "It is I; don't be afraid."
Then they were willing to take him into the boat,
and immediately the boat
reached the shore where they were heading."
John 6:16-21 (NIV)

From that point forward, they "Let Go and Let God" steer their path forward. Laura shared, "We wanted Jesus to be in our boat with us."

Choosing Faith Over Fear

With clarity and focus, Matt and Laura fully surrendered every aspect of their Chicago ministry to God, including housing, income, jobs, food, and safety. Yes, there were bumps in their journey, but each day, they asked their Heavenly Father for the strength and courage to keep pressing forward with His plans.

Thankfully, God connected Matt and Laura with a group of young couples and families who were part of the Church of the Nazarene in Chicago called "Reach 77". This non-traditional group deploys missionary teams to start churches throughout the seventy-seven neighborhoods of Chicago. The teams live in the most disadvantaged neighborhoods, so they can quickly help people in need and share the good news about Jesus!

Members of the "Reach 77" team immediately embraced Laura and Matt. A few couples came alongside them to provide emotional support, answer numerous questions, offer suggestions on housing, etc. These phone and internet acquaintances quickly became trusted friends. They were an answer to their prayers.

Then, another miracle happened. God nudged Pastor James to "get creative" and have the church support Matt and Laura while they served the Lord in Chicago. He shared, "The vision was simple. As missionaries from our local church, they would GO and be the hands and feet of Jesus in inner-city Chicago while our church provided financial support and prayer cover."

After discussions with the church board, Pastor James told Matt and Laura, "Our church is going to send you to Chicago, offset some of your financial burdens, and pray for you while you fulfill the Lord's calling in the inner city." Laura and Matt's hearts filled with gratitude as they praised God for His continued affirmations and support.

"...If God is for us, who can be against us?"
Romans 8:31 (NIV)

A few weeks later, God prompted Pastor James to extend an opportunity for church members to contribute to the upcoming ministry in Chicago. As he described the vision from the pulpit, God immediately touched the hearts of many people gathered in the church that morning. People generously followed God's prompting and made financial pledges to support their journey. God was on the move in a BIG way!

Hope For Your Journey

Pastor James led an emotional and faith-filled "send-off service" the following month, just a few days before they left for the mission field of Chicago. At the end of the service, the young couple came to the front of the sanctuary as friends, family, and church members lovingly encircled them. Together, they prayed and asked God to bless their ministry and provide a constant hedge of protection around this family.

"The Lord bless you and keep you;
the Lord make his face shine on you
and be gracious to you;
the Lord turn his face toward you
and give you peace."
Numbers 6:24-26 (NIV)

Their first week in Chicago was a major culture shock. Since money was tight and they did not have jobs, they squeezed their family into an old 400-square-foot basement apartment. It was a significant change from the comfort of their 2300-square-foot townhome. However, Laura did her best to transition the tiny apartment into a cozy home using the limited furniture and belongings they brought with them. With some creativity, they successfully converted a small closet into a nursery for Camden, who was now nine months old. Despite their cramped space, they praised God and pushed forward.

"For I know the plans I have for you," declares the Lord,
"plans to prosper you and not to harm you,
plans to give you hope and a future."
Jeremiah 29:11 (NIV)

The neighborhood and activities surrounding their apartment, especially at night, were very different compared to their prior environment. There was constant noise from sirens, honking, loud music, people yelling with angry voices, fireworks, and occasional gunshots. From 12 PM to 5 AM, darkness ruled – from drugs to illicit sex to murders and more. It was a far cry from the safe neighborhood they left behind. They prayed for protection daily – and sometimes hourly.

"So do not fear, for I am with you;
do not be dismayed, for I am your God.
I will strengthen you and help you;
I will uphold you with my righteous right hand."
Isaiah 41:10 (NIV)

Choosing Faith Over Fear

Once they settled into their apartment and connected with their "Reach 77" friends, Matt, Laura, and little Camden started taking daily prayer walks around their neighborhood. They asked God to open their eyes, disclose the areas where He wanted them to serve, and reveal job opportunities in their neighborhood.

During their walks, they were surrounded by loneliness, broken lives, and people sleeping on the sidewalks. The smell and stench were sometimes overwhelming. It was heartbreaking, and they thought – Lord, where do we start when there are SO MANY hurting people?

"But God will never forget the needy;
the hope of the afflicted will never perish."
Psalm 9:18 (NIV)

On one walk, Laura noticed a sign advertising an opening for a behavior therapist. Thankfully, God equipped Laura with a degree in psychology and a national board certification in behavior analysis. She applied for the position and was immediately hired. Matt landed a job as a food services manager for the Chicago Cubs. Gratefully, they could split their shifts and generate enough income to offset their expenses. Despite their significant pay cuts, they praised God for their jobs and then turned their attention to the numerous needs in their neighborhood.

Matt shared, "When we started our outreach, we did not know what to expect and specifically who we would be ministering to. So, we opened our hearts, and God allowed us to start listening to the stories of hurting people from all walks of life. When we truly began to listen to their heart-wrenching and painful stories, God allowed us to see people the way Jesus sees people – with love and compassion. It was a life-altering experience."

"But the wisdom that comes from heaven is first of all pure;
then peace-loving, considerate, submissive,
full of mercy and good fruit, impartial and sincere."
James 3:17 (NIV)

While in Chicago, Matt and Laura survived the most challenging yet rewarding time in their lives. They depended entirely on their Heavenly Father as they obeyed His calling – despite the evil and dangers surrounding them. Sadly, violence in the inner city was common. However, they served and prayed in obedience, no matter how uncomfortable the situation appeared. As they followed God's lead, He kept them safe, guarded their hearts and minds, and performed miracle after miracle as He transformed people's lives.

"Do not be anxious about anything, but in every situation,
by prayer and petition, with thanksgiving,
present your requests to God.
And the peace of God, which transcends all understanding,
will guard your hearts and your minds in Christ Jesus."
Philippians 4:6-7 (NIV)

Thankfully, as they trusted God, He faithfully surrounded them with their circle of friends (who became family) from the "Reach 77" team. Together, they loved, encouraged, and prayed for each other 24/7 as they boldly shared the good news about Jesus in the roughest parts of Chicago – even when it was scary, or situations seemed impossible. Through encouraging hugs, prayers, pep talks, texts, and phone calls, their friends gave Laura and Matt the strength and courage they needed to press forward, especially during the really tough times.

Ministry became their way of life. They walked in obedience – no matter how complex, simple, or inconvenient the situations were. Laura shared, "We changed plans regularly to respond to the needs in the neighborhood, whether it be a single mom who needed diapers and food at 10 PM, volunteering for an unplanned early shift at a rehabilitation center, or responding to a neighbor in distress at 2 AM. We viewed these interruptions as divine opportunities to be the hands and feet of Jesus while letting people know God loves them! We knew God had a purpose for those moments."

"And do not forget to do good and to share with others,
for with such sacrifices God is pleased."
Hebrews 13:16 (NIV)

As time passed, they moved into a 700-square-foot apartment and welcomed their second daughter, Hailey, into the world. Despite now being the parents of two young children, they continued to press forward and obey God's calling. They learned to celebrate the small changes God made in people's hearts. Laura shared, "We celebrated the inches of transformation and praised God as we pursued lost and hurting people."

Matt and Laura prayed for protection, along with other "Reach 77" families, as they boldly invited people from their neighborhood into their tiny apartment for Table Life dinners and Life Transformation Groups. Sometimes, up to twenty-five people would attend. Some refugees had never been inside an American home, and it touched their hearts. Matt and Laura also connected, encouraged, and shared the good news about Jesus, from street corners to parks to shelters. Regardless of their week-to-week financial situation, as they generously gave their time and shared their food, God always provided enough funds for their outreach activities.

"And my God will meet all your needs
according to the riches of his glory in Christ Jesus."
Philippians 4:19 (NIV)

Matt and Laura survived month-to-month on a very tight budget as they trusted God with their finances. It was part of their faith journey. However, one month, despite their frugal lifestyle, support from the church, and job income, their debts caught up with them. Their apartment rent was due in two days, and they had no money to cover it.

Then, one day, Matt and Laura's "Reach 77" mentor came to their apartment to check in, see how things were going, and discuss various topics. During the conversation, Matt mentioned they did not have the money to cover this month's rent, but they were faithfully praying and continuing to trust God because He is always faithful.

"Be joyful in hope, patient in affliction, faithful in prayer."
Romans 12:12 (NIV)

When their mentor was ready to leave, Matt walked outside with him and decided to grab their mail. As he quickly thumbed through a small handful of envelopes, they continued to talk. Matt was surprised to see a letter from Laura's aunt and uncle, whom they rarely spoke to due to busy schedules. Then, a miracle happened. When he opened the envelope, he pulled out a check that covered the next five months of rent. WOW – once again, God provided!

"Every good and perfect gift is from above,
coming down from the Father of the heavenly lights,
who does not change like shifting shadows."
James 1:17 (NIV)

Matt and Laura shared, "The miracles we saw firsthand in the inner city of Chicago are numerous and could fill an entire book. Some miracles were big, while others were small – but they were ALL blessings from God."

"Many people did not understand why we left a comfortable life to pursue the ministry in Chicago. However, we were willing to be misunderstood if hurting people could have the chance to hear and feel the hope and love of Jesus. We learned that on the other side of comfort are the amazing miracles God wants to perform!"

They continued, "God loves everyone regardless of their ugly baggage or dirty laundry. He is tirelessly chasing after people who do not know Him or have chosen dark paths. One of the scriptures we embraced was Luke 15:4-7. We held Jesus's words close to our hearts."

"Suppose one of you
has a hundred sheep and loses one of them.
Doesn't he leave the ninety-nine in the open country
and go after the lost sheep until he finds it?
And when he finds it,
he joyfully puts it on his shoulders and goes home.

Then he calls his friends and neighbors together and says,
'Rejoice with me; I have found my lost sheep.'

I tell you that in the same way
there will be more rejoicing in heaven
over one sinner who repents than over ninety-nine
righteous persons who do not need to repent."
Luke 15:4-7 (NIV)

After six years in Chicago, Laura unexpectedly received a call from an employer to come back to Virginia – the school district had a job waiting for her. Laura was shocked since she had not applied for any positions. Matt and Laura immediately knew God's fingerprints were all over this opportunity. Thankfully, Matt's current job was flexible, and he could fulfill his work requirements in Virginia.

God was closing this chapter of their lives through a series of events. It was hard to leave their friends and inner-city ministry, but it was clear their time in Chicago was over. It was time for them to move on and rest.

Choosing Faith Over Fear

A few years later, God called them to serve once again. This time, Matt became the lead pastor of their former church, just as Pastor James had envisioned several years earlier. The following year, Laura became the Next Generation Pastor for the church, serving alongside Matt. Soon, God called her to begin the mandatory steps to become an ordained pastor. She accepted His call and is now taking the required seminary courses.

In closing, they shared, "We are honored God called us to serve in the ministry field once again. We ask you to join us and share the good news about Jesus through your words, actions, and deeds. GO out into your community to spread the hope and love of Jesus! May God be with you as you faithfully follow His lead! Amen!"

"For we are God's handiwork,
created in Christ Jesus to do good works,
which God prepared in advance for us to do."
Ephesians 2:10 (NIV)

Hope For Your Journey

REFLECTION

1. Matt and Laura faithfully followed God as they strived to reach lost and hurting people.

   Take a few deep breaths, close your eyes, and reflect. Can you recall a unique time when you faithfully followed God's prompting or calling? What happened? How did it make you feel?

   _____

   _____

   _____

   _____

   _____

2. Matt and Laura chose to be strong and courageous as they fully trusted God.

   "Have I not commanded you? Be strong and courageous.
   Do not be afraid; do not be discouraged,
   for the Lord your God will be with you wherever you go."
   Joshua 1:9 (NIV)

   Can you recall a bold and courageous step you took WITH God? What happened?

   _____

   _____

   _____

   _____

   _____

   _____

Choosing Faith Over Fear

NEXT STEPS

1. Do you know someone at work or in your neighborhood who is struggling or needs to be encouraged? Would you like to help them? If yes, are you willing to "step out" of your comfort zone and do something?

> *"Carry each other's burdens,*
> *and in this way you will fulfill the law of Christ."*
> *Galatians 6:2 (NIV)*

Some simple ideas to encourage someone might include:

– Pray for them	– Ask them how you can help
– Take them to coffee or tea	– Invite them to a church event
– Stop by and say "hi"	– Give them a plate of cookies
– Listen to them	– Lend a helping hand
– Send a card or text	– Be kind and understanding
– Shovel snow off their driveway	– Give them a hug
– Invite them to lunch or dinner	– Rake their leaves

2. Is the comfort of your lifestyle or fear of failure keeping you from fulfilling a particular project or calling from God? What might happen if you fully trust God and boldly follow His lead?

CLOSING PRAYER

Dear Heavenly Father,

Sometimes, I become so self-absorbed and preoccupied with my personal goals and responsibilities that I fail to notice the lost and hurting people in my neighborhood, at work, and even in my family. Please open my heart, eyes, and mind so I can see what you want me to see and hear what you want me to hear. Help me to "get out of" my comfort zone, shake off my fear, and bravely follow you. I love you! Amen.

Surviving Pancreatic Cancer

*"Be joyful in hope,
patient in affliction, faithful in prayer."
Romans 12:12 (NIV)*

Karen was no stranger to adversity. She was a breast cancer survivor, six years and counting! As a teenager, she watched lung and brain cancer kill her father. Sadly, pancreatic cancer recently engulfed her mom within a matter of weeks. Throughout her life, Karen bravely faced cancer from many angles but never envisioned the upcoming battle she would soon encounter.

After the unexpected death of her mom, Karen was doing her best to settle into a "normal" routine. Thankfully, she had a community of friends who provided support and encouragement. God blessed her with a supportive son, and she prayed daily that her estranged daughter would soon be open to a reconciliation. Karen's divorce after twenty-five years was now in the rearview mirror, and her photography business was growing by leaps and bounds. She was moving forward with her life.

Karen lived in a cozy home in the rolling hills of Northern California. Her house was nestled in the middle of nature, overlooking a beautiful lake, which afforded incredible sunrises and sunsets. Karen was optimistic about her future and had a bucket list of exciting adventures. She planned to "live life to the fullest!" After all, she knew firsthand how fragile life could be.

Unfortunately, life does not always unfold according to our earthly plans. It was New Year's Day 2022. Karen woke up bright and early, just in time to watch a stunning sunrise. She then shared an upbeat post on Facebook, "Wishing everyone a healthy, joyful, and prosperous year ahead!" That afternoon, Karen enjoyed a rejuvenating afternoon hike. She always felt at peace and closest to God when surrounded by nature and His beautiful creations.

*"Let the heavens rejoice, let the earth be glad;
let the sea resound, and all that is in it.
Let the fields be jubilant, and everything in them;
let all the trees of the forest sing for joy."
Psalm 96:11-12 (NIV)*

Despite Karen's optimistic mindset and beautiful surroundings, there was a nagging concern in the back of her mind. For the past few months, she had endured a pressure sensation in her upper right abdomen just below her ribs. The pain would come and go, and sometimes, it was intense. She had seen a few doctors who ran a battery of tests, including bloodwork, an ultrasound, a CT scan, and an MRI scan.

The initial ultrasound scan showed a 1.2 cm small mass (the size of a pea) in her pancreas, but all other tests determined this finding to be an anomaly. The initial diagnosis was gastritis brought on by stress, and a follow-up diagnosis by another doctor indicated she "most likely" had a pulled muscle.

In February 2022, as her abdominal pain became more consistent, additional medical tests were conducted, but once again, everything came back "normal." At this point, her doctor dismissively said, "We have exhausted all our options. The pain may be something you just need to live with." Karen left the doctor's office feeling very uneasy. She sensed something was wrong in her body.

Karen believed in the power of prayer and asked God for guidance and answers. She did not attend a formal church as she preferred connecting with her Heavenly Father each day during her nature and reflection walks. Her friends and family also prayed for her health. Karen's sister, Kathy, faithfully prayed and asked God to heal her sister's pain or help the doctors medically correct the issue.

*"Do not be anxious about anything,
but in every situation,
by prayer and petition, with thanksgiving,
present your requests to God."
Philippians 4:6 (NIV)*

In the Spring of 2022, she was referred to a gastroenterologist as her pain continued. Over the next few months, the doctor conducted an endoscopy and colonoscopy. Both tests were completely "normal."

Hope For Your Journey

However, she still sensed something was wrong and continued to pray for a resolution to her unresolved pain.

Then, one summer evening, Karen experienced a divine intervention, which she believes was a "wake-up call." It had been a long day, and it was dark outside. Since she lived alone, the doors were locked, and the house was secure. As the persistent pressure and pain in her upper abdomen continued, she tried to keep her mind occupied and not worry. On this particular night, she was sitting at the kitchen counter working on some photographs for a client.

Karen shared, "Suddenly, a loud ringing noise interrupted the silence. Startled, I hurried down the hall, following the sound to the guestroom where my mom had stayed when visiting. I quickly opened the door and flipped on the light to find my mom's wind-up alarm clock ringing incessantly by the side of the bed. No one had touched the clock since I placed it there several months earlier."

"I quickly walked over and picked up the clock, trying to turn it off. Nothing I did would stop the ringing. Then, as suddenly as the alarm clock started to ring, it stopped. As I slowly sat the alarm clock back on the bedside table, chills covered my body."

Karen believed the unexplained ringing was a divine, urgent sign to keep advocating for answers regarding the mysterious pain in her abdomen. From that point forward, the clock could no longer keep time.

"Be still, and know that I am God..."
Psalm 46:10 (NIV)

In August 2022, Karen returned to her gastrologist and advocated for herself. She stated the persistent abdomen pressure and pain had not gone away. So, her doctor said, "Let's go back to the basics." He ordered an ultrasound. At the end of the ultrasound exam, the technician explained she would receive the results from her doctor in seven days.

An hour after she left the clinic, her phone rang. It was her doctor. He said, "Karen, the ultrasound found a solid mass in your pancreas. It is 1.2 cm (about the size of a pea.) It is not a cyst. We must do a biopsy.

Karen's mind began to race as she reflected on the ultrasound results from ten months earlier. It also revealed a 1.2 cm mass, but several doctors felt it was an anomaly since the follow-up CT and MRI scans

Surviving Pancreatic Cancer

showed no mass. Then, she quickly thought, "Thank goodness it has not grown."

The following week, Karen had an endoscopic biopsy. The doctor located the tumor in her pancreas and completed the procedure. As she began to come out of sedation, she heard the doctor say, "It is abnormal." A few days later, she received the pathology report. She had pancreatic cancer.

Due to her mother's pancreatic cancer, Karen was fully aware that, in most cases, this type of cancer is a death sentence – it usually metastasizes before diagnosis. To make this sobering statistic worse, Karen knew seven people who had pancreatic cancer over the past eighteen months. The majority of these dear people had already passed away.

The cancerous tumor was located in the mid-body of her pancreas close to the splenic vein. But there was some positive news – the cancerous tumor appeared to be encapsulated and had not metastasized. A PET scan of her entire body revealed no other signs of cancer.

Due to Karen's family history, the medical team also conducted genetic testing to determine if she inherited a mutation linked to pancreatic cancer. Thankfully, based on the currently available testing, the results did not identify any genetic predispositions. She was grateful.

The oncologist team recommended two months and four rounds of intense chemotherapy before surgery. As Karen prepared for the upcoming treatments, she adopted a four-pronged approach.

- The power of prayer!
- Leaning on her community of family and friends.
- Practicing gratitude and praising God for the many blessings in her life.
- Trusting her doctors and medical science.

Soon after Karen received a chemo port, they started her chemo regimen for pancreatic cancer, which the doctors called the "Big Guns Chemo." She was extremely ill after each infusion. Thankfully, she stayed with a dear friend for three or four days after each chemo session.

"Have mercy on me, Lord, for I am faint;
heal me, Lord, for my bones are in agony."
Psalm 6:2 (NIV)

Hope For Your Journey

As she faced the following chemo treatments, Karen surrendered her fears to God and trusted He would heal her through a miracle or the means of medical science. Unfortunately, cancer invoked many worries and "what if" scenarios in her head. With God's help, Karen strived to shift her mindset, maintain a positive outlook, and be grateful for her many blessings.

"So do not fear, for I am with you;
do not be dismayed, for I am your God.
I will strengthen you and help you;
I will uphold you with my righteous right hand."
Isaiah 41:10 (NIV)

Despite the debilitating impacts of chemo (e.g., nausea, neuropathy, extreme exhaustion, weakness, horrible brain fog, impact to bones, etc.) Karen did her best to advocate for herself through research and pointed questions to her doctors. She openly shared her cancer journey on Facebook and asked people to pray for her. Finally, Karen realized her fate was in her Heavenly Father's and doctors' hands. She was at peace with her situation.

"And the peace of God,
which transcends all understanding,
will guard your hearts and your minds in Christ Jesus."
Philippians 4:7 (NIV)

After two months of gut-wrenching chemo treatments, the doctors scheduled her surgery for December 20, 2022 – yes, five days before Christmas. Her surgery was extensive. They removed half of her pancreas, her spleen, the splenic vein, and eleven lymph nodes. She spent Christmas in the hospital and was grateful to be alive! Eight days after surgery, the doctors released her from the hospital, and she continued to recuperate at a dear friend's home.

Then, Karen received the best post-Christmas gift of all. The pathology report revealed NO CANCER spread to her lymph nodes or adjoining organs. Words cannot describe the joy and gratitude that filled her heart!

However, there was a problem. The pathology report also disclosed the chemotherapy treatments did not reduce the size of the tumor. When the tumor was surgically removed, it still contained live, active cancer cells. Subsequently, the chemo treatments were considered a failure. Therefore, the doctors changed the post-operative treatment plan to a different chemo protocol. The treatments would commence as soon as she recovered from surgery.

"Heal me, Lord, and I will be healed;
save me and I will be saved,
for you are the one I praise."
Jeremiah 17:14 (NIV)

In February of 2023, Karen began her second chemotherapy regimen. Unfortunately, due to the cumulative toxins in her system, each treatment became harder and harder on her body. Thankfully, her friends and family faithfully lifted her in prayer and put their "love into action" once again. They drove her to and from chemo appointments, sat with her for test results, called, texted, messaged, and sent cards. Some friends quietly sat with her and held her hand. At no time did she feel alone.

"The Lord sustains them on their sickbed
and restores them from their bed of illness."
Psalm 41:3 (NIV)

Sadly, the adverse effects of the chemo treatments intensified, and each infusion became more toxic. In addition to the horrible side effects Karen previously experienced, the skin on her hands and feet blistered and fell off. She was unable to walk and could not grip anything. It was at this point Karen fully surrendered her pain and loss of control to God.

Despite the unbearable pain, Karen sat on her deck each day, soaking in God's beautiful creations. She shared, "The magnificence of nature was a constant reminder of God's power and love. From the chirping birds to water lapping on the lake's shore to leaves blowing in the wind, I had an unexplained sense of hope!"

"But those who hope in the Lord
will renew their strength.
They will soar on wings like eagles;
they will run and not grow weary,
they will walk and not be faint."
Isaiah 40:31 (NIV)

Hope For Your Journey

In June 2023, Karen received her last chemo infusion. On her final day, the nurses and technicians surrounded her chemo chair and applauded her bravery. They also presented her with a chemo graduation certificate. Karen's heart overflowed with gratitude, and she cried.

The abdominal pain Karen experienced never disappeared. The doctors determined once and for all this pain was not associated with her cancer. She believes God used the pain to get her attention so she could receive the proper medical treatments and fulfill God's purpose for her life here on earth.

Karen shared, "You know your body. If you sense something is not right, it's okay to advocate for yourself and seek additional medical opinions. Trust the whispers from God."

As part of her post-cancer follow-up, Karen has regular blood tests and CT scans. All her follow-up tests to date show she is CANCER-FREE. She is a pancreatic cancer survivor!

Karen is living a life of gratitude. She shared, "Be the light that God created you to be. Love one another. Be the best version of yourself. If there is conflict, make amends and do it now! We are not guaranteed tomorrow. Every moment is precious."

In closing, Karen shared, "I could feel God carrying me throughout my cancer journey, and I will forever be grateful. If you are a skeptic and wonder if miracles exist in our modern world, look no further than me. I am a walking miracle. Praise God!"

"Lord my God, I called to you for help,
and you healed me."
Psalm 30:2 (NIV)

Surviving Pancreatic Cancer

Karen – Six months after her chemo treatments

The Alarm Clock

Hope For Your Journey

REFLECTION

Based on the statistics regarding pancreatic cancer, the human odds were stacked against Karen. However, during her journey, she embraced her faith in God, the power of prayer, and the importance of intercessory prayer (other people praying for us.) God blessed Karen with a miracle and healed her here on earth.

*"Now faith is confidence in what we hope for
and assurance about what we do not see."*
Hebrews 11:1 (NIV)

Pause and Reflect

- Do you have faith and confidence in God?

- Do you believe in the power of prayer?

_____

_____

_____

_____

_____

_____

_____

_____

_____

_____

Surviving Pancreatic Cancer

NEXT STEPS

Karen is grateful for the numerous people who prayed during her cancer journey.

- Do you have someone in your life who will faithfully pray for you?

_____

_____

_____

- Are you faithfully praying for people in your life?

_____

_____

_____

- Are there some steps you want to take to ensure you make "prayer" a daily priority?

_____

_____

_____

CLOSING PRAYER

Dear Heavenly Father,

Thank you for loving me. Thank you for listening to me 24/7, regardless of how big or small my challenges may be. Please remind me to pray every day. I love you. Amen.

Surrounded by Wildfires

"But those who hope in the Lord
will renew their strength.
They will soar on wings like eagles;
they will run and not grow weary,
they will walk and not be faint."
Isaiah 40:31 (NIV)

Life was difficult! Beth recently lost her mother to brain cancer, and the COVID pandemic continued to rage. Her twenty-four-year marriage was unraveling, and the chronic pain in her back was relentless. To further complicate the situation, there were ongoing challenges with her mother's estate and discontent among her siblings. Beth was mentally exhausted.

Despite all the challenges, Beth was grateful for the blessings in her life. Her home was only minutes away from the breathtaking Rocky Mountain National Park. She began each day with a fresh cup of coffee while enjoying the sunrise, gazing at the mountains, and thanking God for His many blessings. She sat in awe as elk and other wildlife quietly passed by and savored the changing seasons from her backyard. Her heart overflowed with gratitude.

"Give thanks to the Lord, for he is good.
His love endures forever."
Psalm 136:1 (NIV)

The summer of 2020 was unseasonably hot and dry in the Colorado Rockies. Dead grass covered the foothills, and the rushing creeks withered to shallow brooks. Due to the extremely arid conditions, Beth and her neighbors prayed for rain and lower temperatures as the fall season drew near. Unfortunately, the dry heat continued with a high risk of fires.

Surrounded by Wildfires

As October approached, a relentless wildfire started in the Rocky Mountain backcountry, likely sparked by a hunter or camper. The fire quickly grew due to the dry and windy conditions. No one could have predicted this fire would soon become the second-largest wildfire in Colorado's recorded history.

As Beth and her husband Sam carefully monitored the situation, the flames rapidly consumed miles and miles of wilderness. Before long, the erratic winds began to push the blaze toward populated areas. Then, one night, the fire "blew up."

While the inferno was still thirty miles away, they suddenly realized their mountain home was in the firestorm's unyielding path. Within hours, officials placed their small town under pre-evacuation orders. Their only escape route consisted of one two-lane road down the mountain.

With tears flowing down her face, Beth prayed while Sam tried to figure out what items to pack. Finally, Beth cried out, "Oh Lord, what do I do?" Overwhelmed by the situation, they quickly gathered a few special items, grabbed key papers, and threw some clothes into suitcases and bags. Running from room to room, they suddenly realized their earthly treasures and material possessions were unimportant when faced with a life-threatening dilemma.

> *"For where your treasure is,*
> *there your heart will be also."*
> *Matthew 6:21 (NIV)*

The first night in their home under the pre-evacuation status was exhausting. The unyielding winds howled as they anxiously waited for fire updates and evacuation guidance. Their hearts jumped every time their phones dinged with an updated text or email. It was awful, but Beth continued to pray.

When morning finally dawned, their neighborhood was intact, but they were not out of danger. The fire was rapidly growing, and a second fire was heading toward the town from the opposite direction. The neighborhood remained on pre-evacuation orders for days as firefighters from several states frantically fought the flames both on the ground and from the air. The relentless and erratic winds minimized the water and fire-retardant drops, making it difficult to create and hold fire lines.

*"Before them fire devours,
behind them a flame blazes.
Before them the land is like the garden of Eden,
behind them, a desert waste..."
Joel 2:3 (NIV)*

Desperate for fire updates, neighbors openly shared information gathered from handheld ham radios and volunteer firefighters. Day after day, the updates painted a grim picture for their small town. Businesses were closed, and families anxiously waited in their homes for directions from the authorities. Unfortunately, due to the extremely dry and windy conditions, a third fire was now burning out of control and heading toward their small community.

Despite the upheaval, Beth continued to pray and placed her hope in the Lord. She chose to keep trusting Him as she sought His peace and comfort. For she knew God would provide for them, whether their earthly house remained, or the flames devoured their home.

*"And my God will meet all your needs
according to the riches of his glory in Christ Jesus."
Philippians 4:19 (NIV)*

As the wildfires raged into a second week, Beth was grateful for her friends and family, who faithfully prayed on their behalf. Each time her faith started to waiver from anxiety and fear, a friend would text a note of encouragement or share a powerful Bible verse. She was thankful for the emotional support God provided through others. His unwavering grace and love sustained her through some of their darkest days.

Not knowing when formal evacuation instructions would finally come, Beth and Sam took short naps during the day, then slept in shifts during the night to carefully monitor the fire alerts. Each time a breaking news announcement blasted on the TV, they had an adrenaline rush. They were mentally and physically exhausted.

The smell of smoke permeated their home as ash covered their roof, driveway, and yard. During the day, the sky filled with dark, billowing smoke. At night, an orange glow from the fires lit the sky. The intense, persistent winds continued to howl, carrying sparks and flames to new areas. Beth faithfully prayed for the firefighters. She also prayed for the animals in peril as they ran for their lives.

Then, on the fourteenth day, the county officials informed the residents that evacuation requirements were now imminent. Evacuations were underway at mile marker sixteen, and their home was just off the road at mile marker twelve. Due to the dense smoke, car headlights were necessary to travel during the day.

Overwhelmed by the notification, Beth prayed, "Lord, I have survived so much loss and mental anguish over the last few years. I can't take any more. I know this is your house, but I ask you to protect it."

At dusk that evening, while they awaited final evacuation orders, the Lord prompted Beth to take a flashlight, go outside, and walk around their home seven times — like Joshua and his army walked around the walls of Jericho (Joshua 6:1-27.) Without hesitation and with complete obedience, Beth immediately threw on her coat, grabbed a flashlight, and went outside to walk around the perimeter of their property.

As she faithfully walked, the flashlight guided her steps while ash the size of snowflakes fell all around her. The strong smell of smoke was overwhelming, and the forceful winds nearly took her breath away. But, determined to be faithful, she continued to walk and pray, "Lord, I know this is YOUR house. If the fire comes up and over the ridge, please protect YOUR home and the barriers I am walking."

" But when you ask, you must believe and not doubt,
because the one who doubts is like a wave of the sea,
blown and tossed by the wind."
James 1:6 (NIV)

After finishing the seventh prayer lap around their property, Beth again thanked her Heavenly Father for His many blessings. Looking up at the orange glow on the surrounding mountains, she coughed from the smoke and rubbed her irritated eyes. Before entering the front door, Beth attempted to brush the ashes from her coat and hair. She was exhausted and needed some quiet time.

About three hours later, Beth was startled when her husband started screaming and frantically running down the basement stairs. Struggling to catch his breath and gather his words, he finally blurted out, "You're not going to believe this. Snow came! We don't have to evacuate!" Sam immediately grabbed Beth and embraced her. They both sobbed as she shouted out, "Thank you, Jesus. Thank you, Jesus!"

Hope For Your Journey

For you see, a couple of hours earlier, for no explained reason, the winds shifted, and fog encased the surrounding mountains. According to the National Weather Service, precipitation was not in the forecast. But suddenly, freezing rain began to fall on the intense fires. Before long, ice and snow blanketed the fields around their home. It was a miracle. The snow was like manna falling from heaven.

With tears of joy, Beth continued to praise our Heavenly Father. She thanked Him for listening and answering the multitude of prayers from people across the country. Her heart overflowed with gratitude for all the people who faithfully prayed over the long two weeks.

> *"Let everything that has breath praise the Lord.*
> *Praise the Lord."*
> *Psalm 150:6 (NIV)*

She then paused to reflect on the families who lost their homes and asked God to be with them as they dealt with their destroyed houses and new reality. Next, Beth thanked God for the firefighters and the state, local, and federal officials who tirelessly worked to extinguish the fires. Finally, she asked God for a special blessing over the exhausted firefighters and their families. She prayed for their continued protection.

But this is not the end of the story, for God is in the restoration business. As a direct result of the fires and other hardships Beth and Sam faced together, God reignited their love and commitment to each other. The fires from afar refined and softened their hardened hearts as they supported each other, for better or worse, during this challenging time. Together, they saw what God can do when we believe, seek His will, and put Him first. Through God's guidance and love, He restored their broken marriage. They recently celebrated their twenty-seventh wedding anniversary. Praise God!

> *"And we know that in all things*
> *God works for the good of those who love him,*
> *who have been called according to his purpose."*
> *Romans 8:28 (NIV)*

In closing, Beth shared, "We serve an awesome God! If you place your hope and faith in Him, He will carry you through life's challenges, heartbreaks, and mistakes. You are a child of God, and He loves you!"

Surrounded by Wildfires

REFLECTION

1. Beth experienced many emotions as the fires raged toward their home. When she felt overwhelmed or afraid, she sought God's peace and comfort by simply talking to Him and asking for help.

   Do you recall a time when you asked God for help? What happened?

   _____

   _____

   _____

   _____

   _____

   _____

   _____

2. Beth and Sam could only pack a few items when they evacuated. What would you pack and why?

   _____

   _____

   _____

   _____

   _____

   _____

   _____

Hope For Your Journey

NEXT STEPS

1. Is there an area in your life where you are afraid, worried, or confused? Take a moment and write your thoughts below.

    _____

    _____

2. Do you want to ask God for help? If yes, you do not need fancy words to pray and talk with Him. He is ready to listen and help you 24/7 with <u>ALL</u> areas of your life.

    Below are a few simple prayers to help you.

    *   Dear God, I am <u>afraid</u> of _____.
        Please take away my fear and help me _____.
        Thank you. Amen.

    *   Dear God, I am <u>worried</u> about_____.
        I know my constant worrying is zapping my energy and not accomplishing anything. Please guide and direct my next steps regarding _____and give me peace. Thank you. Amen.

    *   Dear God, I am <u>confused</u> about _____.
        I know "confusion" does not come from you. Please provide clarity for me regarding _____ and guide my next steps. I trust you. Thank you. Amen.

CLOSING PRAYER

Dear Heavenly Father,

Thank you for listening to my prayers, even when I ramble and probably don't make sense. Thank you for comforting me when I'm sad and helping me when I'm afraid. Thank you for reassuring me when I worry and providing clarity when I am confused. Amen.

The Family I Never Knew

"I can do all things through Christ who strengthens me."
Philippians 4:13 (NKJV)

Angie was happily married and the mother of two boys, Ethan and Zach. Life was great, but she had a gap in her heart – she grew up never knowing her biological father. Angie's husband wanted to help fill this void, so he lovingly purchased an Ancestry DNA kit for Mother's Day 2019 and said, "I know you always wanted to find your father." His thoughtful gift touched Angie's heart as her mind filled with anticipation, excitement, and fear.

To fully grasp Angie's story, we must return to the fall of 1967 in northeastern Pennsylvania. The beautiful autumn leaves were now blanketing the ground in the small town of Montrose, and winter was just around the corner. There was a sixteen-year-old girl named Lois who was struggling in high school due to depression, extreme anxiety, and health challenges.

"Cast all your anxiety on him because he cares for you."
1 Peter 5:7 (NIV)

Despite numerous attempts to overcome her debilitating issues, Lois dropped out of high school during her sophomore year. She had no plans for her future and continued to live at home while struggling with chronic anxiety and depression – challenges that doctors would later diagnose as bipolar disorder. Sadly, at the time, people did not openly discuss or address mental health issues.

As autumn progressed, a man named David came to town with her cousin's boyfriend. Lois was immediately captivated by this man, who was nine years older. They began dating, and Lois fell in love. She believed they were going to be married. He was from Oakland, California (near San Francisco), divorced, and the father of three children: two daughters and one son.

Hope For Your Journey

However, as time passed, Lois decided to break off their relationship. Then, just as quickly as David appeared, he hitchhiked out of town, never knowing Lois was pregnant with his child. She did not have his phone number or address. No one knew how to reach him since the internet, Facebook, and cell phones did not exist. So, from Lois's perspective, the father of her unborn child lived 3,000 miles away, and she would never see him again.

In the 1960s, an unwed, pregnant teenager was considered an outcast of society. Lois's doctor encouraged her to consider adoption, but with her mother's full support, she refused to contemplate this option and never considered an abortion. Despite her emotional challenges and the stigma that hung over her head, Lois loved her unborn baby and was committed to becoming a mother. Thankfully, a loving and supportive family surrounded her on this unplanned journey.

So, at age seventeen, Lois bravely gave birth to a beautiful baby girl. Little Angie lived with her mom and grandmother for the next five years. With the help of devoted aunts and uncles, Angie's grandmother worked hard to provide a stable and loving home. Despite Lois's emotional challenges and erratic outbursts, Angie shared, "I always knew my mom and family loved me."

From an early age, God and the church were cornerstones of Angie's life. She said, "I loved attending Sunday School and Vacation Bible School. I clearly remember asking Jesus to come live in my heart when I was only four years old. Thankfully, throughout my life, my Heavenly Father faithfully carried me. He NEVER left me, regardless of the fears, heartbreaks, and obstacles I faced."

> *Jesus said, "Let the little children come to me,*
> *and do not hinder them,*
> *for the kingdom of heaven belongs to such as these."*
> *Matthew 19:14 (NIV)*

When Angie turned five, her mother married a younger man. Her new stepfather was only thirteen years older than Angie, but he strived to be a loving father and was always kind. Unfortunately, he was also a "big talker," which led to broken promises and financial hardships. Subsequently, they lived in poverty. On several occasions, her parents could not pay their monthly rent, so they frequently moved due to eviction notices from their landlords.

The Family I Never Knew

Despite their financial hardships, when Angie was seven, her mom became pregnant and had another daughter. Lois loved the girls, but her erratic mood swings created a volatile home life. Angie looked forward to spending time with her grandmother, aunts, and uncles. They brought joy and stability to her life. Sunday school and church continued to be pillars of solitude for little Angie. She loved singing and listening to stories about God.

"...In this world you will have trouble.
But take heart! I have overcome the world."
John 16:33 (NIV)

When Angie was in the fourth grade, she recalls living in a house with her mother and stepfather that was basically "falling down." They had no hot water in their home, and food was scarce. Due to her mother's unpredictable behavior and their financial pressures, her parents separated several times. Life was not easy. Then, unexpectedly, her mother became pregnant once again, giving Angie a second little sister.

Around this time, Angie began to experience a nagging curiosity about her biological father. So, one day, she wrote him a letter. Angie only knew his name and that he lived somewhere in the Oakland/San Francisco area of California — facts that would remain lodged in her mind as the years rolled forward. She never mailed the letter since she did not have his address or phone number.

Sadly, there were times when Angie's mom was unable to care for her children as she dealt with emotional challenges, which sometimes required lengthy stays in the hospital. The situation was further complicated due to her mother and stepfather's unstable marriage. So, off and on over the years, Angie and her sisters lived with their aunt and uncle where they were surrounded by love.

She shared, "Despite my situation, I knew God was with me. He always placed the right people around me — just when I needed them. My Heavenly Father faithfully provided a loving foundation for my life."

She continued, "Then, one day, my world came crashing down. A few days before my twelfth birthday, I spent a few nights with my aunt and uncle for a fun visit, then returned to my mom and stepfather's house to prepare for my birthday sleepover party. I was so excited. But just before our celebration, we received gut-wrenching news. My

Hope For Your Journey

aunt, uncle, and one of their sons had been brutally murdered in their home by my cousin's boyfriend. I was devastated."

"I later learned that neighbors told the police they had seen a young girl staying at my aunt and uncle's house. Since the police could not locate "the girl," they frantically searched the woods behind the house, fearing she was dead or kidnapped. That "young girl" was me – God spared my life."

"God is our refuge and strength,
an ever-present help in trouble."
Psalm 46:1 (NIV)

The following few years were an emotional roller coaster as Angie strived to keep moving forward while silently carrying the weight of suppressed feelings. Trauma and grief therapy were not openly discussed or readily accessible in the early 1980s, especially in a small town. The situation was further complicated when Angie's parents divorced. Her mother, with the help of family members, struggled to provide a home for her three daughters. Life was difficult as Angie tried to focus on school and maintain excellent grades – despite her unstable home life.

Unfortunately, Angie's suppressed and unresolved feelings finally caught up with her and led to a failed suicide attempt when she was sixteen years old. Angie shared, "I'm not sure why I wrote a note and tried to commit suicide with diet pills – perhaps I did it for attention or a cry for help. Regardless of the reason, God immediately surrounded me with "just the right people I needed" to carry me through high school and ensure I remembered God was with me – no matter what challenges I faced."

Angie joined the church choir with a friend as she looked for ways to stabilize her life. This decision was a big step since she was quiet and shy. Angie shared, "Singing in the choir and attending church filled me with joy and gave me hope – despite the upheaval in my life. When I was in church, it felt right. I knew it was where I was supposed to be."

"Sing to God, sing in praise of his name,
extol him who rides on the cloud;
rejoice before him—his name is the Lord.

A father to the fatherless, a defender of widows,
is God in his holy dwelling."
Psalm 68:4-5 (NIV)

The Family I Never Knew

She continued, "As I held on to my faith in God, He met me right where I was and made my path easier. My best friend's mom became my advocate and loved me like a daughter. She supported me as I mourned my grandmother's death during my junior year of high school. She encouraged me as I dealt with the day-to-day pressures of school and held me accountable for achieving good grades. I will forever be grateful."

"And my God will meet all your needs
according to the riches of his glory in Christ Jesus."
Philippians 4:19 (NIV)

After graduation, Angie headed off to college, thanks to student loans and grants. The university was over six hours from home, but she quickly adapted to the new environment. However, the open gaps surrounding her biological dad and curiosity about unknown siblings continued to hover in the back of her mind.

Then, one day during her freshman year, Angie walked into the college library and unexpectedly discovered a collection of phone books from all over the United States (remember, social media and the internet were not accessible to the general public in the 1980s.) Suddenly, her mind began to race as she thought, "Could these phone books be the link to locating my father?"

With that fleeting thought, Angie said a quick prayer, took a deep breath, and began searching through the shelves of California phone books, striving to find the San Francisco / Oakland directory. Suddenly, her eyes caught a glimpse of the right book. Was she finally one step closer to finding her biological father?

As she bravely reached for the thick book, Angie's heart pounded with excitement, and her mind quickly filled with fear about the unknown. Could she be opening Pandora's Box? Despite the fear, she began fanning through the pages, anxiously searching for her father's name.

Suddenly, there it was! Angie finally found her father's name in black and white – unfortunately, she found his name over and over again. Overwhelmed by the sheer number of entries for people with the same name, she stopped. The fear of making cold calls to strangers and concerns about the unknown quickly took control of her mind and actions.

Hope For Your Journey

Angie slowly closed the directory and placed it back on the shelf. She decided to take no further action that day. Angie was mentally exhausted as her mind continued to fill with "what-if scenarios" and unanswered questions. Then she thought, "Maybe someday I will get answers."

A few weeks later, Angie started dating a young man who attended the same college. She shared, "After we dated for a while, my boyfriend's parents (who lived close to the college) began to embrace me like a member of their family. Once again, God blessed me with the right people at the right time – just when I needed them. My boyfriend and I attended church with his parents and enjoyed Sunday dinners at their home. They were the "All-American Family" I always dreamed about. God knew their calm and mellow approach to life was what I desperately needed."

After graduation and for the next two decades, Angie faced many highs and lows. She married her college sweetheart, had a good job, endured the painful journey of infertility, enjoyed the joys of adoption, lived through the heartbreak of divorce, and survived the challenges of being a single mother of a child with Oppositional Defiant Disorder (ODD) coupled with Attention Deficit / Hyperactivity Disorder (ADHD). But through it all, God was ALWAYS with her and provided the strength and hope she needed to keep pressing forward. Angie's faith remained steadfast and unshakable.

> *"Be joyful in hope, patient in affliction, faithful in prayer."*
> *Romans 12:12 (NIV)*

Despite the upheaval in Angie's life, she proactively and gladly served in many roles at the local church. She particularly enjoyed working as a Sunday School teacher and Youth Director. Yet, even with her faith in God and service to others, Angie's mind still wondered about her biological father and siblings. The tugging on her heart never left.

Then, in 2008, when Angie was forty years old, her life took an unexpected turn. Against all odds and prior infertility challenges, she became pregnant. Angie and Joe, the new love of her life, welcomed a little boy into their lives. Together, they created a loving home for their two children. Life was great, but she still had a gap in her heart and yearned to know her biological father.

The Family I Never Knew

Angie's husband wanted to help fill this void, so he lovingly purchased an Ancestry DNA kit for Mother's Day 2019 and said, "I know you always wanted to find your father." His thoughtful gift touched Angie's heart as her mind filled with anticipation, excitement, and fear once again.

It was time for Angie to "take a leap of faith with God" to find her biological father! She shared, "I was nervous yet excited as I tried to manage my hopes and expectations. What if I don't find my father? What if I do find my father?"

As her mind bounced from thought to thought, Angie prayed for God's will and strength before gently opening the DNA kit. She carefully followed the instructions in the kit, spit into the little tube, placed the tube in the provided envelope, mailed it, and waited on the Lord.

> *"But they that wait upon the Lord*
> *shall renew their strength;*
> *they shall mount up with wings as eagles;*
> *they shall run, and not be weary;*
> *and they shall walk, and not faint."*
> *Isaiah 40:31 (KJV)*

A few weeks later, an email appeared in Angie's mailbox titled, "Your Ancestry DNA results are in!" She was at work – but could not stand the suspense. So, she took a deep breath, said a quick prayer, opened the Ancestry app on her phone, then clicked the button for DNA matches.

Suddenly, the DNA information popped up. At the top of the list was a "possible sibling" match with a woman named Carol – and she had the same last name as Angie's biological father. Angie quickly thought, "Is this my sister?"

Angie began to shake. Overcome by emotions, she decided to take a short walk outside, compose herself, and call her mother. When her mom answered the phone, she blurted out, "I think I found my sister." Angie's mother was supportive and encouraging.

That evening, she thanked God, asked for His continued guidance, and then wrote a message to Carol via the Ancestry app. After some introductory words, she shared, "I had my DNA analysis done in hopes of finding information about my birth father. It has always been the one big mystery in my life. You are my closest DNA match, and you have

Hope For Your Journey

my father's last name. I hope you will be willing to chat and help me. Thanks so much."

The following day, Angie received a response from Carol. "Hi. What is your dad's name? If he is related to me, I'll try to help you."

"Do not withhold good from those to whom it is due,
when it is in your power to act."
Proverbs 3:27 (NIV)

Shaking, Angie thought, "Oh my goodness, I am about to tell this woman she has a sister." After taking a deep breath and saying a short prayer, she typed, "Thank you for writing back! His name is David. I think he was born in the early forties. I was born in 1968."

Later that day, Carol responded, "David is my dad. What is your mom's name? I will ask my dad if he knew your mom or knew about you." Angie quickly responded with the details about her mother, including how and where her mom met David.

Carol warmly and openly responded, saying she would talk with her father, then shared, "...We have a half-brother named Keith from Dad's second marriage. My Mom was Dad's first wife – they had two children, my sister and me. My sister passed away from cancer in 2013. As far as we knew, we were Dad's only three kids."

The next day, Angie again heard from Carol, "This has been hard for all of us. I talked to Dad last night. He recalls the trip to Pennsylvania but did not know about you. Let's just say he's in shock and not quite ready for a phone call."

At that point, Angie and Carol shared personal contact information and talked on the phone a few weeks later. Angie shared, "It was God's plan for me to find my father – as it turned out, he was quite easy to find thanks to Carol's compassionate and kind heart. Carol is a lovely person, and I will always be grateful."

Angie became Facebook friends with Carol and her father. She respected her father's desire not to connect via the phone while he processed this surprising information and new situation. Finally, eight weeks later, Angie's father broke his silence. She shared, "I will never forget my father's Facebook post on my birthday. It read, "Happy

Birthday. I love you." These simple words meant a great deal to me – and finally filled a hole in my heart."

"He will turn the hearts of the parents to their children,
and the hearts of the children to their parents..."
Malachi 4:6 (NIV)

Before long, Carol invited Angie to join her "new family" for Thanksgiving. At that point, Angie had still not spoken on the phone with her father. Despite that fact, and with her husband's full support, Angie jumped at the opportunity and said yes. She booked a flight and hotel, counted the days before the trip, and waited. She knew God would be with her as he opened this new chapter.

"Yet the Lord longs to be gracious to you;
therefore he will rise up to show you compassion.
For the Lord is a God of justice.
Blessed are all who wait for him!"
Isaiah 30:18 (NIV)

Angie was terrified as she boarded the flight a few days before Thanksgiving and checked into the hotel. After procrastinating in the hotel room the following morning, she finally prayed, picked up the cell phone at 2 PM, and called her father for the first time. Angie nervously introduced herself and asked for directions to his home. She shared, "Despite the awkward situation, my dad was kind and immediately put me at ease. It was wonderful to hear his voice for the very first time."

On her way to his house, she stopped and bought flowers. When she rang the doorbell, her father came to the door, greeted her with a big hug, and said, "I'm so happy you are here." Angie said, "I instantly felt comfortable and loved."

She continued, "My Dad and I spent the rest of the afternoon visiting and shopping together at Walmart. It just felt normal. Then, that evening, I met Carol for the first time. We hugged as if we had known each other our entire lives and laughed as we discovered our similarities. The entire weekend was perfect, and I felt blessed. I am so grateful my dad and "new family" are a part of my life. Praise God!"

In closing, Angie shared, "My journey to finally meet "the family I never knew" was full of hardships and heartbreaks. I am not sure why I faced so many adversities in my life, but through it all, I held on to my faith in God, and He never left me. God always showed up and made my path easier. He placed the right people in my life when I needed them. For you see, with God, ALL things are possible."

Angie

The Family I Never Knew

REFLECTION

Despite Angie's challenges and adversities, she continued to have faith. She never gave up on God! Time after time, He showed up and made her path easier, even when the path seemed impossible.

Do you recall a time when God showed up to carry you through a challenge or adversity? What happened? How did He help you?

Hope For Your Journey

NEXT STEPS

As we saw in Angie's story, God will meet you right where you are, regardless of your challenges, adversities, or past traumas.

Do you want to take a leap of faith? Do you want God to help you with your challenges and adversities?

If you answered yes, God is available 24/7 to meet you right where you are, regardless of your situation or things you have done. You do not need fancy words – simply pray this prayer:

Dear God,
I need your help.
Please guide my life and help me with _____.
Thank you. Amen.

CLOSING PRAYER

Dear Heavenly Father,

Thank you for caring about me and loving me right where I am. Thank you for listening when I cry out for help and surrounding me with people to make my journey easier. Please help me to continually look up to you for guidance and direction as I push forward.

I love you. Amen.

Pause and Reflect

"This is the day that the Lord has made;
let us rejoice and be glad in it."
Psalm 118:24 (ESV)

It was a brisk fall morning at Rehoboth Beach. The sun glistened on the water as Monsour enjoyed a quiet walk along the shore. He watched the seagulls gliding in the air and the waves billowing on the sand as he contemplated life and reflected on his many blessings. He was thankful for God's creations.

Continuing his walk, Monsour encountered a special moment that would stay with him forever. He noticed a family peacefully sitting on the beach while their baby girl played and crawled on the sand. He paused to enjoy the moment from a respectful distance. Monsour had always hoped to be a father, but that blessing was not part of his journey.

Suddenly, this sweet baby started to stand up on her wobbly little legs all by herself as her parents provided positive reinforcement. Then, after she swayed to the left and right, Monsour witnessed this child take her very first steps before gently falling on her tush.

Her parents cheered, and Monsour's heart filled with love as he embraced the significance of the moment. While he was not a father, God blessed him with the experience of this child's first steps. Without saying a word or intruding on the family's special moment, Monsour quietly moved on. As he began to reflect, he realized this child would never know she positively and profoundly impacted his life.

Monsour was grateful, and his heart was full of love. He experienced this child's first steps because he <u>chose</u> to "be present" and "live in the moment." Due to his choice, he received a blessing that would last a lifetime.

"Every good and perfect gift is from above…."
James 1:17 (NIV)

Hope For Your Journey

We live in a rapidly paced world. Cell phones, live streaming, and Alexa are just a few of our fixations with today's "on-demand" technology. But, if we are not careful, the convenience of technology or preoccupation with our jobs will steal our ability to experience the special times in life — moments God provides to give us hope for our journey.

Monsour at Rehoboth Beach

Pause and Reflect

REFLECTION

Can you recall a time when you put down the phone, turned off the TV, and chose to be present with your family and friends?

If yes, what happened? How did you feel? How did they react?

Hope For Your Journey

NEXT STEPS

As we juggle the demands in our daily lives, finding time to "be present" can be challenging.

What are some ways you can choose to be present today?

_____

_____

_____

_____

_____

_____

_____

_____

CLOSING PRAYER

Dear Heavenly Father,

Thank you for the special moments you provide as I journey through life. I am grateful. Amen.

A Wild Teenager – But God Had a Plan!

"For I know the plans I have for you,"
declares the Lord,
"plans to prosper you and not to harm you,
plans to give you hope and a future."
Jeremiah 29:11 (NIV)

Camelot was a wild teenager. Her motto was "The more rules you break, the more friends you have." Booze, partying, cigarettes, and boys – they were what she lived for. Compulsive lying quickly became the cornerstone of her personality. Camelot was out of control, and nothing phased her. Then, one day, life caught up with her – and her world came crashing down.

Camelot was born in Greenville, South Carolina, in the 1970s. Her parents struggled to make ends meet. Thankfully, they were able to rent a small, single-wide trailer to keep them warm and buy enough food for every meal. As Camelot describes it, "We were poor." Financial pressures and other challenges put a strain on her parents' marriage, so they divorced when she was only two years old. Life was tough.

After the divorce, Camelot's single mother did her best to provide a good home for her daughter despite significant financial concerns. Together, they moved into a tiny house next to her mother's cousin, making it easy for Camelot to have a babysitter while her mom worked. She spent time with her father every other weekend, but the back and forth from home to home was confusing, especially after her dad married her stepmother.

"Cast all your anxiety on him because he cares for you."
1 Peter 5:7 (NIV)

When Camelot was five years old, her mother began working as an administrative assistant for a successful businessman, who happened to be a millionaire. As time evolved, her mother started dating her new boss. Camelot said, "My mom's boss was very tall and nice. He took us to Disneyworld and bought me a huge Mickey Mouse. I was so excited."

When she was seven, her mother married her boss. From that point forward, Camelot's life drastically changed. She said, "My life became a true rags to riches story. I was suddenly living in a big house with a huge bedroom, and our financial challenges disappeared. We had a lovely housekeeper named Ruth, who came in early every morning to cook and clean. She also cared for me when I was not in school. I loved Ruth – she became an important and special friend."

"Perfume and incense bring joy to the heart,
and the pleasantness of a friend
springs from their heartfelt advice."
Proverbs 27:9 (NIV)

In addition to the changes in her living environment, Camelot's step-father transformed other areas of her life. Education was important to him, and he quickly realized Camelot could not read, write, or complete simple math since she did not know her numbers. Her skill gaps concerned him, so he immediately intervened and began investing in her education.

Her parents enrolled her in a private Episcopal school as she entered the second grade. A Christian school was an interesting choice, given her stepfather was Jewish. Camelot immediately flourished in her new learning environment thanks to a caring teacher named Mrs. Riley and the extra tutoring she received. By the end of the school year, Camelot was reading, writing, and accomplishing math at the third-grade level.

Camelot's school accomplishments helped build her self-confidence, yet despite her achievements, there were emotional voids in her life. Her stepfather ran his new family and household like a business – no emotions were allowed. Camelot said, "If I became emotional, I was told to leave the room and collect myself. So, when I needed to cry, I would crawl under a shelf in my bedroom closet – it became my safe place. I kept some of my favorite little books under that shelf. They made me feel good as I learned to console myself."

"Fathers, do not embitter your children,
or they will become discouraged."
Colossians 3:21 (NIV)

By the time Camelot was ten, she felt trapped in an exhausting cycle of going back and forth between her parents' homes. She shared, "My parent's lifestyles were drastically different. Dad and his wife lived a happy but extremely modest life and were actively involved in church. On the other hand, when I was with my mom and stepfather, I felt like I lived on Park Avenue and was expected to behave accordingly. It was hard to meet the different expectations of each home. I was never allowed to relax and just be me. I had to pretend to be two different people to survive and fit in. The situation was overwhelming."

Her stepmother was concerned about her and began to pray. As she prayed, she saw Camelot crying. Suddenly, a comforting angel appeared and gently touched Camelot, saying," Don't worry. Everything will be OK." This vision and gift from God would carry her father and step-mother through the next twelve tumultuous years.

"Praise the Lord, you his angels,
you mighty ones who do his bidding,
who obey his word."
Psalm 103:20 (NIV)

Then, one weekend, Camelot's mom and stepdad decided to take a quick trip to their beachfront condo in Myrtle Beach. Like any young girl, Camelot wanted to go to the beach rather than spend an uneventful weekend with her father and stepmom. When her father arrived at the house, she reluctantly got in his old truck, and they began to drive away.

Suddenly, Camelot looked at her father and bluntly said, "James, I never want to see you again." She had never called her father by his first name but wanted his full attention. With those words, her father sadly turned the truck around and returned Camelot to her mother.

Camelot loved her father but was relieved she could finally stop going back and forth from house to house. She was tired of trying to be the kid everyone thought she should be. Her father was heartbroken, but he continued to pray for his daughter. Later that year, he adopted a little boy with his wife as Camelot embarked on some painful years.

When Camelot entered the seventh grade, her world began to spiral out of control. Her self-esteem was already low when she decided to get a new short hairstyle with a perm. The results were devastating and embarrassing for a twelve-year-old girl.

Hope For Your Journey

Camelot shared, "I looked like a poodle. I was mortified and embarrassed as I walked the school halls and heard the snickers and laughter. I just wanted to have friends and fit in versus being bullied. I could not show any emotions at home, so I silently retreated inside my head." Sadly, a level of depression began to take hold in Camelot's mind, and she did not know where to turn or what to do. She knew who God was but did not have a relationship with him or know how to pray.

"The Lord is close to the brokenhearted
and saves those who are crushed in spirit."
Psalm 34:18 (NIV)

That same year, Camelot dealt with additional family pressures as her father sued for custody. She had not seen her dad since their awkward conversation in his old truck almost two years earlier. Camelot knew she had treated her father poorly and was wrong. After the court proceedings, the judge required her to spend four hours a year at Christmas with her father and stepmom – she was OK with the decision.

Her life continued to slide in the wrong direction during her eighth-grade year. Someone told a lie about Camelot, but she never discovered what mean or hurtful things were said. Sadly, all the eighth-grade girls bonded together against Camelot. They shunned her and refused to talk to her for the entire school year. She wanted to fit in and have friends instead of feeling like an outcast.

"God is our refuge and strength,
an ever-present help in trouble."
Psalm 46:1 (NIV)

As isolation and depression took a strong hold on her life – tears and sadness filled her heart, and she did not know where to turn. Her relationship with both sets of parents was superficial, and she did not have a relationship with God. Then, the unthinkable happened. Ruth, Camelot's sweet friend and caregiver, passed away. She shared, "I was devastated. At this point, my life began to come off the rails."

As she entered high school, an older cousin introduced her to a group of wild girls, and they started to hang out. Sadly, this circle of friends was a bad influence on her. Striving to fit in, Camelot learned and shared a dirty song. Almost overnight, she became one of the most popular girls in the group, all because she did something "against the acceptable norms and rules." For the first time in a long time, her depression began to lift. She belonged and had friends, something she had always wished for. Camelot liked how she felt, but Satan was on the prowl.

"Be alert and of sober mind. Your enemy the devil
prowls around like a roaring lion
looking for someone to devour."
1 Peter 5:8 (NIV)

As the school year progressed, Camelot's academic and social abilities grew. Due to the emotional pain she experienced growing up, especially during middle school, Camelot developed a high level of emotional intelligence. She became keenly aware of the feelings, motives, and fears of the teenagers around her and noticed students who endured bullying or struggled to fit in. She did not want other people to experience the pain she had previously felt as an outsider.

So, Camelot started to talk with everyone at school without judging, striving to weave outsiders into areas where they could fit in and belong – a skill God would eventually leverage for His kingdom. To her surprise, her willingness to include others increased her popularity. Helping "hurting people" made her feel good.

Unfortunately, Satan continued to prowl around in Camelot's life and deteriorate her basic value system while she strived to increase her acceptance and popularity. By age fifteen, Camelot was among the most popular girls on campus due in part to her softball and field hockey athletic abilities as well as her willingness to go against acceptable social norms. Her motto was "The more rules you break, the more friends you have."

"If anyone, then, knows the good they ought to do
and doesn't do it, it is sin for them."
James 4:17 (NIV)

Booze, cigarettes, boys, and partying – they were what she lived for. Compulsive lying quickly became the cornerstone of her personality. Sneaking out of the house to party late at night was part of her routine. If caught lying or breaking the rules, Camelot could make herself cry to squeeze out of punishments or consequences.

Hope For Your Journey

> *"The Lord detests lying lips,*
> *but he delights in people who are trustworthy."*
> *Proverbs 12:22 (NIV)*

Despite her partying and deceitful ways, Camelot managed to get good grades, graduated from high school, and received an acceptance letter to her number one college choice. She shared, "I purposely selected the college because I heard there were lots of drugs. Both sets of parents had plans for me, but no one ever bothered to ask me. I was out of control, and nothing phased me."

Camelot's first year of college was wild. She was "all in" for the party lifestyle. Since alcohol made her sick, she transitioned to a variety of drugs, including mushrooms and ecstasy. Camelot missed classes and couldn't care less about school. Her sole focus was getting high with friends and hanging out with many boyfriends. She leveraged her compulsive lying skills when her parents asked questions about school or her lifestyle – especially after failing a few classes. Trouble began to follow her.

Then, one evening, when she was partying, a good-looking guy named Sam pulled up in a truck. He was a mechanic and into the party lifestyle, including drugs. So, Camelot and several other girls got in the back of his truck.

She ended up going on a double date that same evening – one of her friends went out with Sam, and she joined them with another guy. As the night ended, Camelot told her friend, "The man you went on a date with tonight – I'm going to marry him." She did not see Sam again until her sophomore year, over twelve months later.

> *"I will instruct you and teach you*
> *in the way you should go;*
> *I will counsel you with my loving eye on you."*
> *Psalm 32:8 (NIV)*

During Camelot's sophomore year, her crazy lifestyle and partying intensified. Then, one night, when she was partying with her boyfriend at a house near the college campus, she ran into Sam, and her heart skipped a beat! As they chatted, her boyfriend ran off with another girl. Sam looked at Camelot and said, "Do you want to take a ride?" She firmly replied, "I will not get involved with you until I officially terminate my relationship with my boyfriend – even though he just ran off with someone else, I want to do things right."

The following week, Sam reached out to Camelot, and they went on a first date at the local skating rink. As a couple, they clicked and started dating each other exclusively while continuing to party and do drugs. Sam was kind, attentive, and compassionate – all qualities she sought in a partner.

Camelot continued to struggle in college due to her lackadaisical attitude. Attending classes and focusing on homework took time away from partying and hanging out. Getting a college education was the furthest thing from her mind.

> *"Whatever you do, work at it with all your heart,*
> *as working for the Lord, not for human masters."*
> Colossians 3:23 (NIV)

During the fall break, Camelot went home to celebrate Thanksgiving. Her parents openly expressed their concerns regarding her grades. They strongly encouraged her to focus on her education, which they were financing. Camelot effectively leveraged her compulsive lying skills to reassure her parents that she would apply herself, study hard, and turn things around. She never mentioned her new boyfriend during their conversations.

In reality, Camelot had no intention of adhering to her parents' firm advice. Her goal was to return to college so she could party and see Sam. She was surprised at how much she missed her boyfriend during their short time apart.

Without Camelot's knowledge, her mother quietly investigated her activities when she returned to school. She learned her daughter was dating a local mechanic named Sam, who was not attending college. Her mom feared Camelot might run off with this young man and never complete her degree.

Then, one night, Camelot left the dorms with Sam to go partying. When they returned at 2 AM, her roommate said, "You need to call your mom ASAP. She has called several times and is very upset with you." (Remember: cell phones were not available in the early 1990s.)

Hope For Your Journey

Camelot turned to Sam and said, "I'm going to talk with my mom. She is probably going to make me choose between my family and you. Are you in this relationship with me? I need to know." Sam firmly responded he was committed to their relationship. So, with that knowledge, Camelot dialed the phone.

When her agitated mother answered the phone, she firmly said, "If you continue the relationship with Sam, don't bother to come home." Camelot responded, "Okay. I am not leaving him."

With that six-word response, Camelot's mother and stepfather disowned Camelot, and the world as she knew it came crashing down. They immediately cut off her credit card access, took her car, and stopped all college funding, including tuition, room, and boarding payments.

With limited options and no money, Camelot moved into Sam's single-wide trailer. She had come full circle. The only things she now owned were a few items from her dorm room and some winter clothes. She was once again poor but grateful to have Sam in her life.

When Camelot called her father to share the latest dilemma, he immediately sent some grocery cards to ensure she had enough food. His thoughtful and kind gesture touched her heart. Her father also invited Sam and Camelot to join them for Christmas, but they were too preoccupied with parties. When Sam was not at work, all they cared about was partying and taking drugs.

A few weeks later, Sam and Camelot spent Christmas with his family. Sam's Christian mother welcomed her with open arms, gave her $250 as a Christmas gift, and said, "You are part of our family!" The kind words and gestures were important to Camelot since she continued to have an overwhelming need to be accepted and fit in.

As the months passed, Camelot continued to live with Sam as their partying and drug use continued. Then, out of the blue, her stepfather offered to fly her to Washington, DC, for a face-to-face discussion. Intrigued, she accepted his offer. During their conversation, her stepdad said he would cover her tuition and books if she attended summer school and received straight A's. In addition, he would continue to pay her college tuition and cover her books if she completed this goal.

Camelot accepted his offer, attended summer school in cut-off jeans (since she could not afford summer clothes), and received a 4.0 GPA. She was a good student when she applied herself. Unfortunately, her stepfather refused to cover her future college expenses. His company filed for bankruptcy, and he had significant marriage issues due to his infidelity. So, Camelot quit school again and began working for a printing business. While at work, a friend and co-worker (the daughter of a Nazarene minister) began to share her faith and tell her about God.

He said to them, "Go into all the world
and preach the gospel to all creation."
Mark 16:15 (NIV)

Then, one night, several friends were partying in Sam's single-wide trailer, including the son of a Seventh-Day Adventist preacher. For some reason, this friend brought his Bible to the party. While getting high, Camelot debated with the young man whether the Sabbath was on Saturday or Sunday. He was so high on drugs that he forgot his Bible when he left.

The next day, when Sam was at work, Camelot noticed the Bible on the table. For some odd reason, she thought, "I wonder if the Bible has an ending." With that thought, she picked up the Bible, flipped through the pages, and began reading the last book of the Bible called Revelation.

Suddenly, in a panic, she called Sam at work and said, "Sam, you need to come home!" When he asked why, she replied, "Because Jesus is coming back!" With that response, Sam said, "Honey, don't move. I will be right home." He was concerned Camelot had taken some bad drugs and was hallucinating.

When he came home, they had a serious conversation about the Bible. Then Sam said, "We should probably go to church at some point." Four weeks later, after a hard night of partying, smoking, and getting high, Camelot and Sam woke up at 7 AM on a Sunday, grabbed breakfast, and headed to church.

Camelot only knew of one Baptist church close to the trailer, so that is where they went. Church had already started when they arrived, and the huge sanctuary was full of people. They smelled of cigarette smoke. Camelot wore an extremely short one-piece jumper, which was inappropriate for a conservative church service in 1994 – but it

Hope For Your Journey

was the only nice clothing she owned. Thankfully, a kind usher greeted them with open arms and kindly led them to open seats.

The usher seated them in the second row from the front of the church. They were uncomfortable with their seating arrangement but did not want to move or make a scene. They noticed several TV cameras behind them recording the service and felt boxed in for the next hour. But God now had their undivided attention, with no drugs, booze, or cigarettes to distract them.

As the minister began to share the morning sermon, it suddenly became clear it was not a coincidence they chose this day to attend church together. They came to church by their own free will, but God planned the words they would hear that day. The pastor read scripture after scripture from the Bible. He talked about the sins of sexual immorality, abuse of alcohol, and the harmful impacts of illegal drugs on your body. He shared that God has a purpose for ALL our lives. His message – GOD'S MESSAGE – touched their hearts.

As the service began to close, the pastor shared, "God will meet you right where you are regardless of your past decisions, lifestyle, or messed up life. All are welcome to join the kingdom of God. Jesus already paid the price for your sins on the cross – He died for your sins. You simply need to accept Jesus as your personal Savior, turn away from your past and sinful lifestyles, and run into the loving arms of Jesus. He is patiently and lovingly waiting for you!"

"For God so loved the world
that he gave his one and only Son,
that whoever believes in him
shall not perish but have eternal life.

For God did not send his Son into the world
to condemn the world,
but to save the world through him."
John 3:16-17 (NIV)

As the church organist and pianist began to play the old hymn, "Just As I Am," the pastor opened the altars and invited people to come forward if they wanted to be obedient to God's calling and the purpose for their lives. There was no pressure from the pastor. At this point, Sam leaned over to Camelot and whispered, "Do you want to go up there?" She replied, "I guess we could."

A Wild Teenager – But God Had a Plan!

Suddenly, they stood up together and stepped out in faith, making their way to the front of the church. That morning, they turned away from their current lifestyle and accepted Jesus as their personal Savior. God immediately met them right where they were and began transforming their lives. He had a purpose and exciting plans for their future.

"And we know that in all things God works
for the good of those who love him,
who have been called according to his purpose."
Romans 8:28 (NIV)

They were no longer the same people when they left the church. As they drove home in Sam's old truck, he turned to Camelot and said, "I guess we should get married. Will you marry me?" She immediately said yes.

God delivered them from their drug and alcohol addictions that day, for you see, with God, ALL things are possible. They never experienced drug withdrawals or desired to use drugs again. They flushed their drugs down the toilet and poured the bottles of alcohol down the drain. They never looked back.

"I waited patiently for the Lord;
he turned to me and heard my cry.

He lifted me out of the slimy pit,
out of the mud and mire;
he set my feet on a rock
and gave me a firm place to stand.

He put a new song in my mouth,
a hymn of praise to our God."
Psalm 40:1-3 (NIV)

That afternoon, they called Sam's mother. She was thrilled with their decision and how God was moving in their lives. They told his mom they planned to get married on Saturday, and she embraced their decision. She gave them $250 to cover their wedding expenses for Camelot's dress, Sam's tuxedo, and a hotel for their wedding night.

Camelot then called her father and shared the day's amazing events and their plans to get married on Saturday. He was thrilled. She then asked her father to give her away at the wedding, and he lovingly said yes!

*"Trust in the Lord with all your heart
and lean not on your own understanding;
in all your ways submit to him,
and he will make your paths straight."*
Proverbs 3:5-6 (NIV)

The following few days were a whirlwind as the wedding plans quickly came together. Sam's mother recommended they get married at her Methodist church. Thankfully, her pastor was available on Saturday and agreed to marry them. They completed marital counseling with the pastor on Tuesday and Thursday. On Wednesday afternoon, Sam's mother and a few family members joined Camelot to search for a wedding dress. After covering the cost of Sam's tuxedo and the hotel for their wedding night, she had exactly $150 set aside for a dress.

Typically, you must order wedding gowns several months in advance. Sadly, the first bridal shop laughed when Camelot explained she needed a wedding dress for Saturday. The second bridal shop was more compassionate but said they could not help her. They recommended she go to JC Penney's and find a pretty white dress for the ceremony. Camelot was a bit sad and disappointed.

Before leaving the bridal shop, they brainstormed potential stores that might have a wedding dress available for purchase in the next forty-eight hours. While they chatted, the shop's phone rang and interrupted their conversation. As the saleswoman listened intently to the person on the phone, her mouth dropped open.

Since it was now dinnertime and the sales associate was on the phone, they started to walk out of the store, unsure of their next steps. Suddenly, the woman held up her index finger and shouted, "Wait!" Perplexed, they stopped and walked back toward the counter.

Then God performed an amazing miracle in Camelot's life! The saleswoman shared, "The phone call was from a young woman who just canceled her wedding dress. Since the dress was altered, I cannot return it. Do you want to try it on?" Camelot immediately replied, "YES!"

The woman escorted Camelot into a big, elegant room encircled by mirrors. In the corner stood a beautiful yet modest wedding dress hanging perfectly on a mannequin. It was the type of dress she envisioned for her wedding day. The sales associate gently unzipped the dress, carefully removed it from the manikin, and handed it to her.

Camelot was ecstatic as she slipped into the dress and admired it in the mirrors. The gorgeous dress fit perfectly!

When Camelot inquired about the cost of the dress, the woman shared, "Since the young woman already paid for the dress and no longer wants it, there is no charge. However, there is an outstanding alteration fee of $150. If you pay the fee, the dress is yours." Camelot thought, "WOW – the exact amount of money I have." She realized this dress was a special gift from God!

"Let us rejoice and be glad
and give him glory!
For the wedding of the Lamb has come,
and his bride has made herself ready.
Fine linen, bright and clean,
was given her to wear."
Revelation 19:7-9 (NIV)

That Saturday, Camelot married Sam in a modest yet perfect wedding. As promised, her father showed up and walked her down the aisle. She was sorry her mother was not there for their special day, but this was not the end of their story.

When they attended church the following weekend, Camelot and Sam wanted to quit smoking, but they were struggling to stop their habit. As new Christians, they were unsure how to pray, so they talked to God the way they spoke to other people, simply praying, "Lord, make us hate smoking." With that prayer, they broke their cigarettes in half and threw them away.

The next day, Camelot was still craving cigarettes, so she purchased a pack with her lunch money. As she took her first drag off a cigarette, she started coughing and felt nauseated. That same day, Sam asked a co-worker if he could have a cigarette. He took one puff off the cigarette and immediately felt sick. They never touched cigarettes again. God answered their prayer.

During her first year as a Christian, Camelot craved to learn about God and the Bible. She faithfully read God's word and attended various Bible studies. The more she learned about her Heavenly Father, the more she wanted to know. Camelot prayed for mentors as she strived to deepen her relationship with God. God always placed the right people in her life just when she needed them.

Hope For Your Journey

Camelot shared her testimony (story) at a small church the following year. She openly discussed how God rescued her from a party lifestyle, including heavy drugs and lies that spiraled out of control. She also shared how God blessed her with a beautiful wedding dress and the love of her life.

"Whoever acknowledges me before others,
I will also acknowledge before my father in heaven."
Matthew 10:32 (NIV)

After Camelot spoke, a young woman approached her and asked, "By chance, did you get your wedding dress on a Wednesday night last September?" Camelot was surprised by her question and responded yes, then shared the name of the bridal salon.

The woman then replied, "That was my dress. We had canceled our wedding a few weeks earlier. While preparing to attend a Wednesday evening church service, I suddenly felt I should cancel the dress, so I called the store. When I talked to the saleswoman, she explained your situation and asked permission to give you the dress. I said yes." God brought the wedding dress story full circle and blessed both women. Their meeting was not a coincidence.

The following year, Camelot learned she was pregnant. After many prayers, she called her mother. During their conversation, she shared the news about her marriage to Sam. She also revealed they were expecting a baby.

By this time, her mother had divorced her stepfather due to his infidelity, but she was now struggling with an alcohol addiction. Despite their past conflicts, Camelot loved her mother and had compassion for her. She lovingly extended an olive branch and asked her mom to join them for the birth of their daughter. This call was the first step on their long road to a complete reconciliation.

As time passed, she began to serve in various capacities in her local church. Then, one day, Camelot shared a devotional at a women's Valentine event. On that day, God tugged on her heart. She felt He was calling her into full-time ministry, but she didn't know what to do or what next steps to take.

Camelot briefly mentioned this feeling to her pastor's wife and thought she heard the following response," The only way you can serve in

A Wild Teenager – But God Had a Plan!

ministry is as a church secretary since you are a woman." Camelot was perplexed and figured her original comment was misunderstood – she took no further action.

She finally finished her bachelor's degree in education and began teaching middle school mathematics. During this time, Camelot actively supported the children's programs at her church and started teaching "Kids' Church" on Wednesday nights. After a few weeks in her new role, the children's pastor followed her out the door and said, "Are you sure God has not called you to be a pastor?"

This call to become a full-time minister kept tugging at her heart. As she prayed for clarity, God placed two amazing mentors in her life: Pastor Vic Bright and Pastor Kerry Willis. With their guidance, Sam's complete support, and many prayers, Camelot left the teaching profession to fill a full-time Christian ministry position at her church. Before long, she began taking seminary classes and eventually became an ordained minister.

Today, Pastor Camelot is the lead pastor of a church in Virginia. She shared, "God used many people throughout my life, from various Christian denominations, to point me in the right direction. He had a purpose for my life and never gave up on me. Despite the many challenges I faced throughout my childhood and the poor decisions I made during my teenage years – God kept chasing after me. He has performed numerous miracles throughout my life, and I will forever be grateful."

> *"You intended to harm me,*
> *but God intended it for good to accomplish*
> *what is now being done, the saving of many lives."*
> *Genesis 50:20 (NIV)*

She continued, "A few years after I became an ordained minister, I requested a copy of the service when Sam and I accepted Jesus as our Savior. I was shocked to hear the pastor's words throughout the service when I listened to the message. They were different than what I recalled. Toward the end of the service, he invited couples who felt called into full-time ministry to come forward. We never heard those words, but we faithfully went forward. God always had a plan for our lives – He patiently waited for us to be obedient!"

Hope For Your Journey

In closing, she shared, "Sam and I have been happily married for thirty years – he is a true gift from God. He has faithfully supported me through the ups and downs of life. Thankfully, God is our stronghold now and forever. For you see, WITH God, ALL things are possible!"

**Camelot and Sam's
First Church Service Together**

**Pastor Camelot and Sam
Happily Married for Thirty Years**

A Wild Teenager – But God Had a Plan!

REFLECTION

In Camelot's relentless desire to "belong" and "fit in," Satan took advantage of her. He urged her to make bad decisions, leading her down his slippery slope. Thankfully, God kept reaching out to Camelot through miracles and various people He placed in her life. She finally looked up and said yes to Him. She now belongs to God.

Be careful! Open your eyes and pay attention to your surroundings and your path. Keep your eyes on God, for Satan is prowling around in his quest to destroy you.

Pause and Reflect:

1. In your desire to "fit in" and "belong," have you ever compromised your values? If yes, what happened?

_____

_____

_____

_____

_____

2. As you look back on your life, can you see the times or places when God was reaching out and carrying you?

_____

_____

_____

_____

_____

Hope For Your Journey

NEXT STEPS

1. Regardless of your painful past or poor decisions, God is ALWAYS waiting for you with open arms. He will meet you right where you are! You can whisper this prayer 24/7 with <u>complete assurance</u> that God is listening to you:

    Dear God, please help me with _____.
    I can no longer do this on my own.
    Thank you. Amen.

2. As we saw throughout Camelot's story, family conflicts, separations, and divorces are painful. As a child or teenager, did you live through your parents' divorce or family conflicts? Are you still harboring some resentment or unresolved feelings?

    There is good news. You can share your feelings with God right now – He will listen to you. God will begin to heal your emotional wounds and repair broken relationships. Trust Him!

CLOSING PRAYER

Dear Heavenly Father,

Life is not easy, and I am tired of trying to lead my own life. Please forgive me for the mistakes and poor decisions I have made. Please guide and direct my thoughts and decisions going forward. I love you. Amen.

God Comforts Us Through Others

"Therefore encourage one another
and build each other up..."
1 Thessalonians 5:11 (NIV)

It was June 2020. Within a matter of months, life around the world drastically changed due to the COVID-19 pandemic. Thousands of people were dying each day, and hospitals were overwhelmed. The world as we knew it seemed to be slipping away.

Despite the horrible state of the world, Sandy knew God was in control, and she chose to place her trust in Him. For you see, just eighteen months earlier, God faithfully carried her through a trying time, including a cancer diagnosis and a complicated hysterectomy. When the doctors operated, they found no cancer, and Sandy fully recovered. She had seen firsthand how God performs miracles.

"God is our refuge and strength,
an ever-present help in trouble."
Psalm 46:1 (NIV)

With the world turning upside down, Sandy strived to maintain some level of normalcy in her life. She walked three miles every morning, creating a unique quiet time with her Heavenly Father. She was grateful for this special time as it gave her strength and peace for the upcoming day. Sandy was also working through a Beth Moore Bible Study and journaling new insights about various Bible verses.

On June 4th, as she was studying the Book of James, Sandy was perplexed by the following Bible verse, which she had read many times before:

"Consider it pure joy, my brothers and sisters,
whenever you face trials of many kinds,
because you know that the testing of your faith
produces perseverance."
James 1:2-3 (NIV)

Hope For Your Journey

Sandy thought (as many of us would think), "I don't want to face trials from Satan. Let's pray for blessings and good stuff. Trials are never fun." But in retrospect, a few weeks later, she realized God was preparing her for an upcoming "trial" she never anticipated.

It was June 9th, just five days after she read James 1:2-3. Sandy felt great as she finished her makeup and headed for work to lead an online training session. Most of the offices in her building were empty due to the pandemic, so she was not concerned about COVID.

Since Sandy lived in a small community, only five minutes from her office, she came home for lunch that day and enjoyed some leftover salad. Before long, she began suffering from severe abdominal pain. Despite walking around, her pain did not subside. Sandy feared she might have food poisoning, so she "called in sick" and went to bed.

Unfortunately, as the hours passed, her pain intensified. Sandy's typically flat stomach was now significantly bloated – she looked six months pregnant. To make matters worse, she could no longer urinate and sensed something was horribly wrong.

She tried to persevere since COVID cases inundated their small community hospital. Sandy begged her Heavenly Father to relieve the pain, but He did not immediately answer her prayers. Reluctantly, she asked her husband, Craig, to drive her to the emergency room (ER) despite the pandemic and her fear of needles and tubes. She could no longer tolerate the intense agony.

Due to COVID restrictions, Craig could not stay with Sandy in the ER. She was on her own. He reluctantly dropped her off according to the required protocol, closely monitored his cell phone, and prayed. When Sandy entered the waiting room, she saw sick, masked people everywhere. The ER staff tried to enforce social distancing, but space and staff were limited.

Sandy tried to be brave in the waiting room while asking God to relieve the pain. She desperately needed to lie down, but no beds or gurneys were available. At this point, getting COVID was the least of her concerns. An hour later, Sandy called Craig and asked him to pick her up. She was unable to sit for hours waiting to see a doctor.

She endured a horrible night as her symptoms intensified. The following morning, Craig again dropped Sandy off at the ER. Thankfully, she was the only patient in the waiting room – it was the first of many miracles to follow. Within minutes, she saw a doctor. He immediately ordered blood work and ran a CT scan on her abdomen. By 10:30 AM, a surgeon came into the ER room with concerning news.

Sandy was in serious condition. She had a bowel obstruction, and the doctor recommended immediate surgery. Abdominal adhesions from her prior surgery were strangling her small intestines. Sandy had been praying for relief, so without hesitation, she said, "Let's do it." She believed surgery was an answer to her prayers.

> *"But when you ask, you must believe and not doubt,*
> *because the one who doubts is like a wave of the sea,*
> *blown and tossed by the wind."*
> *James 1:6 (NIV)*

Scheduling Sandy's emergency surgery was difficult since the hospital was beyond capacity and had other emergency surgeries. The nearest hospital was ninety miles away and also beyond capacity. As the staff diligently worked on the situation, Sandy leaned on her Heavenly Father and waited as she quietly suffered on an ER gurney. She did not know why this was happening but remained steadfast in her faith.

> *"But they that wait upon the Lord*
> *shall renew their strength;*
> *they shall mount up with wings as eagles;*
> *they shall run, and not be weary;*
> *and they shall walk, and not faint."*
> *Isaiah 40:31 (KJV)*

By late afternoon, an operating room nurse named Shirley was preparing her for surgery. Shirley suddenly realized she knew Sandy's husband, a respected real estate agent in town. Enthusiastically, she said, "Call Craig and tell him I will take good care of you in the operating room. I have his phone number and will update him during your surgery. He is welcome to call me anytime." This random connection and her kind words grabbed Sandy's heart. It gave her an immediate sense of peace. She knew God was with her.

As they rolled her into the operating room, Sandy took a deep breath and quietly asked God to be with her during the surgery. While the operating team took care of last-minute details, she realized the anesthesiologist also knew her husband. This insight calmed her nerves. And then,

Hope For Your Journey

another miracle happened. Just before they sedated her, Dr. Stemmer, a well-respected surgeon, walked into the room to assist with her surgery. His presence immediately comforted Sandy as she peacefully drifted into a deep sleep from the anesthesia.

"Do not be anxious about anything,
but in every situation,
by prayer and petition, with thanksgiving,
present your requests to God.

And the peace of God,
which transcends all understanding,
will guard your hearts and your minds in Christ Jesus."
Philippians 4:6-7 (NIV)

Sandy's surgery proved to be more complicated than anticipated. Her situation was life-threatening. Not only did she have a severe bowel obstruction, but a ten-inch section of her small bowel was full of deadly gangrene and had to be removed. It was a miracle she was alive and did not require a colostomy bag. During the surgery, the doctors also extracted her inflamed appendix and several complex adhesions in her abdomen.

The emergency surgery saved Sandy's life, but she remained in serious condition, with numerous wires and tubes protruding from her body to keep her alive. The skilled nursing staff provided 24/7 care as they strived to minimize her pain, monitor her vitals, and ensure the various tubes functioned correctly and remained free of infection. Sandy's NG Tube from her nose to her stomach was extremely painful. It removed fluids and gas from her stomach while minimizing pressure on her abdomen.

Over the next nine days, God stayed close to Sandy while she recovered in the hospital without family visitations due to the pandemic. Despite the situation, God encouraged her physically, emotionally, and spiritually through several compassionate nurses who faithfully went the "extra mile." They became the hands and feet of Jesus.

"Carry each other's burdens, and in this way
you will fulfill the law of Christ."
Galatians 6:2 (NIV)

God Comforts Us Through Others

A few days after her surgery, Sandy became more alert, and some nurses helped her slowly get out of bed and sit in a chair. They celebrated her progress. The next day, she took a short walk despite all the tubes and wires. The nursing team cheered as she carefully placed one foot in front of the other while clenching her IV pole. They encouraged her heart and made her smile. She was grateful.

While lying in bed after her walk, God nudged her to be proactive and step out in faith. Since talking was difficult due to the NG tube, she texted Craig and asked him to bring her Bible, Beth Moore Study Guide, and journal to the hospital's front desk. Sandy knew reading God's word would comfort her and hoped having the Bible near her bed would also witness to others.

> *"Trust in the Lord with all your heart*
> *and lean not on your own understanding;*
> *in all your ways submit to him,*
> *and he will make your paths straight."*
> *Proverbs 3:5-6 (NIV)*

Sandy shared, "Having my Bible, study guide, and journal with me was a significant source of comfort. When I started to focus on my pain, fears, and isolation, the Bible and powerful verses always pointed me back to God."

Four days after her surgery, some of Sandy's body functions began to return. She thanked God as nurses removed a few tubes. However, the painful NG tube remained in place, negatively impacting her ability to converse with nurses or talk on the phone. Her talking challenges intensified feelings of isolation and loneliness. Sandy was frustrated and asked God for strength.

> *"Be strong and take heart,*
> *all you who hope in the Lord."*
> *Psalm 31:24 (NIV)*

That evening, a night nurse named Alicia noticed the Bible and study guide beside Sandy's bed. She said, "Oh, I'm a Christian too. I did a Bible study on the book of James." A few moments later, Alicia asked, "Can I pray for you?" Sandy immediately shook her head up and down.

Despite the COVID pandemic, Alicia reached out to hold Sandy's hand while she prayed. It was the first time someone touched Sandy without

Hope For Your Journey

gloves since her hospitalization. God's spiritual touch through Alicia was an unexpected blessing, and she was again grateful.

> *"A new command I give you: Love one another.*
> *As I have loved you,*
> *so you must love one another."*
> *John 13:34 (NIV)*

Sandy soon learned that family and friends all over the country were praying for her complete recovery. She was particularly touched that her nephew, Derreck, and his family prayed that a caring staff would surround and support her. God answered this prayer over and over again. Sandy praised and thanked the Lord for His compassion.

Despite God's presence and her faith, Sandy was still human. As the day progressed, her anxiety about needles and tubes went into "high gear." When she saw the doctor that evening, Sandy begged him to remove the NG tube due to the pain and inability to talk. The doctor said, "No. You are still unable to eat. It will be very painful if we remove the tube early and then need to re-insert it. We need to leave it in one more day."

While Sandy desperately wanted the tube out of her nose, she began to "stress out" as she thought about the pain she would experience when the doctor removed the tube the following day. Anxiety and fear started to consume her. Thankfully, Sandy recognized the situation and asked God to intervene. She asked for His peace throughout the night while she embraced the following Bible verse.

> *"Let the morning bring me word*
> *of your unfailing love,*
> *for I have put my trust in you.*
> *Show me the way I should go,*
> *for to you I entrust my life."*
> *Psalm 143:8 (NIV)*

Then, another miracle happened. At 4:30 AM, the pain from Sandy's NG tube woke her up. Suddenly, without human intervention, the tube "just fell out" of her nose. Sandy shared, "That morning, God's unfailing love met me in my hospital room, removed the tube, and took my fear away. The touch of my Great Physician!"

God Comforts Us Through Others

"I love the Lord, for he heard my voice;
he heard my cry for mercy.
Because he turned his ear to me,
I will call on him as long as I live."
Psalm 116:1-2 (NIV)

Sandy could finally talk without pain. Wearing a mask, she walked around the hospital ward several times while carefully holding her IV pole. Looking around, she realized the hospital was overflowing with people in serious condition from COVID and other ailments. Yet, despite the stressful situation surrounding the nurses 24/7, they continued to provide loving, compassionate care for Sandy. God's love shined through the nursing team, and she was grateful.

"Praise be to the God and Father of our Lord Jesus Christ,
the Father of compassion and the God of all comfort,
who comforts us in all our troubles, so that we can comfort those
in any trouble with the comfort we ourselves receive from God."
2 Corinthians 1:3-5 (NIV)

That evening, Sandy was allowed to have liquids after a week without food. They brought her an awful, icky white soup. She asked one of the nurses if she could get a different soup, and the nurse replied, "I'll send your waiter right in." They both laughed as they enjoyed a human moment. A few minutes later, the nurse brought Sandy some chicken broth, and she was grateful.

Later that night, she enjoyed a good night's sleep. She was feeling better, regaining strength, and was ready to go home. Her son and his wife, who lived four hours away, had joined Craig several days earlier. Together, they continued to pray for Sandy's full recovery.

The following day, over a week after surgery, Sandy's blood work finally looked good. She was confident the doctor would let her go home. Unfortunately, that was not the case. Her doctor firmly said, "Gangrene is very serious. If I had not done the surgery in time, we would not be having this conversation. We need to go slowly. You are doing well, considering the circumstances."

When the doctor left her room, Sandy was upset and cried. Jamie, one of her nurses, came over to Sandy's bed, hugged her, and suggested she pray for God's will. Then, Jamie compassionately recapped

Hope For Your Journey

what the doctor said so she could relay the situation to Craig over the phone.

That evening, Sandy finally graduated to a soft liquid diet, another big step in her recovery. Despite her progress, the isolation continued to haunt her. She was lonely and wanted to be home with her family.

Then, a tough but excellent nurse named Carolyn came into her room. She looked at Sandy and said, "What do you think your son would do if he were in your place?" Carolyn paused momentarily, then said, "Do you have a cell phone?" Sandy replied, "Yes!" Nurse Carolyn then replied, "Can you FaceTime? – – Well?"

Sandy shared, "That ah-ha moment immediately cheered me up and pulled me out of my self-centered focus. Once again, God showed me compassion through a nurse." She continued, "Our FaceTime visit that evening was great. It was a blessing for both me and my family. As we said good night, I told them the doctor might release me in a day or two. Everyone was grateful."

The next morning was Sandy's ninth day in the hospital. Her IV was now failing, and the nurse needed to replace it. She pleaded with the nurse, whose name was Faith. "Oh please, no. Not another IV." Faith listened to her request, gave her space, and returned at 2 PM. She then spent a long time with Sandy, asking questions, reviewing various reports, and updating the hospital records.

When the doctor came in at 4 PM, as part of his daily rounds, he looked at Sandy and said, "Well, would you like to go home?" Sandy was surprised and excited. It was evident that Nurse Faith had stepped in and advocated on her behalf. God was in control.

A sweet nurse washed Sandy's hair before she left the hospital. This kind gesture meant a great deal as she regained some dignity after all the poking and prodding. Then, a nurse helped Sandy dress and showed her how to navigate the two abdominal tubes that would remain for the next few weeks. She was ready to go home.

By 5:40 PM, the hospital staff officially released Sandy. That evening, she enjoyed homemade soup on her back patio surrounded by loving family. Sandy said, "It was the best meal I ever had – and an evening I will never forget." Through a series of miracles, she was alive and home.

*"Praise the Lord, my soul,
and forget not all his benefits—*

*who forgives all your sins
and heals all your diseases,*

*who redeems your life from the pit
and crowns you with love and compassion,*

*who satisfies your desires with good things
so that your youth is renewed like the eagle's."
Psalm 103:2-5 (NIV)*

Sandy shared, "God is good, ALL THE TIME! He truly listens to the cries of our hearts. Over and over, He used nurses and other people to compassionately and lovingly care for me. It was tough going through this crisis without my husband and family by my side. However, at every turn, I knew God was with me. He was in control of my situation."

Sandy continued, "Reflecting on my journey, I can clearly see the times God carried and encouraged me. Through each trial from the adversary, my faith in my Heavenly Father grew stronger and stronger. He never left me. I will forever be grateful for His kindness, miracles, and the wonderful nursing staff who lovingly cared for me. I am SO thankful God saved me. To God be the glory! Amen!"

Hope For Your Journey

Sandy is enjoying life!

God Comforts Us Through Others

REFLECTION

Throughout Sandy's story, it was clear she had a relationship with God. She sought His wisdom, guidance, and comfort each day through prayer, reading the Bible, and interacting with the people He placed in her life.

How can you strengthen your relationship with God?

NEXT STEPS

As we saw in Sandy's story, God will meet you right where you are, regardless of your circumstances. Are you struggling with a health problem, relationship, addiction, or other issue today? Do you want or need God's help?

If yes, pray this simple yet powerful prayer:

Dear God,
Thank you for loving me. I am struggling with _____ and need your help today. Please guide and direct me to make decisions that are pleasing to you. Please surround me with people who will support and help me as I strive to resolve my challenges. Thank you. I love you. Amen.

CLOSING PRAYER

Dear Heavenly Father,

Thank you for listening to my cries for help and guiding my path. Thank you for using people around me to encourage and help me on my journey. You are an awesome God, and I love you. Amen.

A Weight Loss Journey – And So Much More

"Cast all your anxiety on him
because he cares for you."
1 Peter 5:7 (NIV)

God cares about ALL aspects of our lives…yes, even our "weight loss" challenges.

Crystal was happily married and raising two adorable girls. Her part-time job as a Children's Pastor provided flexibility to support the church while fulfilling family responsibilities. She also enjoyed managing a successful, home-based scrapbooking business. Crystal was active, healthy, and thin. Life was great!

Then, in 2005, all aspects of Crystal's life began to shift. As tithing diminished in her congregation, her church reluctantly eliminated five paid positions, leaving Crystal without a job. While disappointed, she faithfully remained in the church as an active volunteer.

Family finances were tight without the part-time pastor income, so Crystal was grateful when she landed a job at a children's gym. Unfortunately, she experienced a freak accident while working at her new job. Crystal had a trampoline accident and hit the concrete. She severely injured her back and compacted her spine. For the next year, she could not work and suffered from chronic, exhausting pain.

Thankfully, her chronic pain subsided after months of prayer and physical rehabilitation. She was grateful and soon found a flexible, part-time job. Just as things were looking up and she started working with a trainer, another freak accident occurred. Crystal fell down a flight of stairs, significantly injuring her knee and ankles. She was discouraged and unable to exercise.

"So we fix our eyes not on what is seen,
but on what is unseen, since what is seen is temporary,
but what is unseen is eternal."
2 Corinthians 4:18 (NIV)

Hope For Your Journey

Subsequently, as Crystal started the slow healing process once again, she began to comfort herself with food, resulting in weight gain. She wore specific types of clothing, so her increase in weight was not easily detected. Her faith in God never wavered, but she began to encourage herself with large volumes of food that contained a lot of carbohydrates (carbs.) Bread, pasta, chips, french fries, Cheetos, and potatoes made her happy – at least while she was eating them.

During Crystal's recovery, other parts of her life began to fall apart. Their sweet youngest daughter, Bridget, began to "hang out" with a group of friends who were a bad influence. Her loving demeanor quickly changed, and she became angry most of the time, but there was no sign of alcohol or drugs. The situation soon spiraled out of control when they learned Bridget posted online comments and pictures about her desire to commit suicide.

After many prayers and some miracles, Bridget was admitted to a local psychiatric hospital for "at-risk teens." The intense in-hospital program made a big difference. Once the doctors were comfortable with Bridget's progress, they transitioned her to a highly structured outpatient program that included evenings and nights at home with her family. Finally, after months of ups and downs, Bridget turned the corner. God answered their prayers and saved their daughter.

> *"But when you ask, you must believe and not doubt,*
> *because the one who doubts is like a wave of the sea,*
> *blown and tossed by the wind."*
> *James 1:6 (NIV)*

During this scary and stressful time, Crystal prayed for help. As she lovingly poured time and energy into her family, she ignored her personal health and mental well-being. She shared, "There was no time for me to exercise, cook healthy meals, or re-energize. I was in survival mode. On most days, I just strived to get through my "to-do" list of doctor appointments, insurance issues, financial challenges, and work commitments."

Stress-eating became part of Crystal's normal lifestyle as she added five pounds every few months. Before long, poor eating habits began to "take a toll" on her body. She was constantly exhausted. Doctors placed her on numerous medications for high blood pressure, blood sugar, acid reflux, allergies, asthma, and other ailments.

A Weight Loss Journey – And So Much More

She shared, "Carbs and sugar made me feel better as I was stuffing my face – food became a momentary escape from the pressures of my life. As I increased the amount of food to obtain my short-term "carb fixes," I started experiencing sugar spikes followed by energy crashes. The ups and downs were hard on my body, and I was constantly exhausted. Unfortunately, I was poorly educated on nutrition and did not understand that sugar and carbs were addicting."

While Crystal regularly sought God for wisdom, she did not fully grasp the power and strength freely available from our Heavenly Father. She shared, "I unknowingly restricted my prayers to God. It never dawned on me that God wanted ALL parts of my life to be healthy and whole. He wanted me, and all of us, to be healthy physically, spiritually, mentally, emotionally, socially, financially, and occupationally / vocationally."

> *"Look to the Lord and his strength;*
> *seek his face always."*
> *1 Chronicles 16:11 (NIV)*

Just as things began to settle down, Crystal and her husband faced challenges with their aging parents, who lived over 1500 miles away. Then, out of the blue, their daughter Bridget began to experience significant health issues. She was diagnosed with postural orthostatic tachycardia syndrome (POTS), which affects the body's automatic functions. Crystal's stress eating intensified as she became her daughter's primary caregiver while working part-time.

Fast food became part of Crystal's daily routine, topped off with large amounts of late-night carbs. One of her favorite stress relievers was a bag of potato chips dipped in peanut butter. Before long, she gained seventy pounds, but sadly, this was not the end of her weight challenges. Her excessive weight began to affect every aspect of her life. Her body ached all the time. She could no longer kneel, had difficulty getting off the couch, and it was hard to bend over without losing her balance.

As her family's financial burdens grew, additional difficulties surfaced. Their oldest daughter, Rebecca, fell and had a severe concussion. Then, Crystal's husband received an alarming cancer diagnosis. Family and friends joined in prayer and asked God for a miracle. Bill's doctors performed surgery to remove the cancerous tumor and were shocked when test results revealed all lymph nodes were clean and

Hope For Your Journey

he required no further treatments. Crystal was keenly aware God was with them on their crazy journey, and she was grateful.

"Do not be anxious about anything,
but in every situation, by prayer and petition,
with thanksgiving, present your requests to God."
Philippians 4:6 (NIV)

When Crystal finally came up for air, she was stunned to discover they had accumulated significant financial debt within six months. While in crisis mode, they ignored their credit card spending. Reluctantly, they refinanced their house to offset over $45,000 in credit card debt.

Then, one day, a dear friend sent her a note that read, "I love you dearly and hate to say this, but I am worried about your weight gain." Crystal knew this note came from a place of love and graciously internalized the message.

The scale now showed 242 pounds. Crystal had gained ninety-two pounds and barely fit into her size twenty-two pants. Her knees and ankles ached, and the numerous medications left her lethargic. The daily temptation to eat large amounts of unhealthy food was taking a toll on her life. Something had to change, but she did not know where to turn or what to do. Thankfully, God intervened and met her right where she was.

"No temptation has overtaken you
except what is common to mankind.
And God is faithful; he will not let you be tempted
beyond what you can bear. But when you are tempted,
he will also provide a way out so that you can endure it."
1 Corinthians 10:13 (NIV)

After many ups and downs, the supplier for Crystal's home business filed for bankruptcy, creating an immediate and unforeseen loss of income. She immediately prayed to God and asked for help. He heard her prayers and quickly leveraged the situation as a "catalyst for change" in Crystal's life.

"This is the confidence we have in approaching God:
That if we ask anything according to his will, he hears us."
1 John 5:14 (NIV)

A Weight Loss Journey – And So Much More

A former business associate soon joined a health product company and asked Crystal to join her team. Somewhat shocked, Crystal laughed at the thought of selling health products at 242 pounds but was quietly intrigued. She thought, "God must have a sense of humor!" Then she paused and thought, "Or, is He closing a chapter of my life and opening a new one?"

With an open mind, she prayed for guidance and God's will for her life. After many discussions with her husband, Crystal took a leap of faith and joined the health company. This new job was the first of many doors God opened as He helped Crystal transform her life.

Over the next several months, Crystal attended conferences and online training about nutrition supplements and healthy eating. She learned about the vitamins, nutrients, and minerals our bodies require to function as God intended. Crystal became educated on the shocking side effects of junk food and the harmful impact unhealthy carbs and sugar can have on our physical and emotional well-being. God had her full attention, but now what? How could she stop "stress eating?" She still weighed 242 pounds and was consuming large amounts of food.

> *"No discipline seems pleasant at the time, but painful.*
> *Later on, however, it produces a harvest*
> *of righteousness and peace for*
> *those who have been trained by it."*
> *Hebrews 12:11 (NIV)*

Crystal decided to try her company's nutrient supplements and began drinking the recommended amount of daily water. Within a month, her energy increased, she no longer needed daily naps to offset her exhaustion, and her significant joint pain disappeared.

God soon opened another door and connected Crystal with a local prayer ministry. Over the next six years, He surrounded her with people deeply rooted in the "power of healing prayer." As people prayed for Crystal, doctors noticed improvements in her health. They slowly stopped previously prescribed medications for blood pressure, blood sugar, allergies, and acid reflux. She was excited and grateful.

However, there was still a major issue. Crystal was not losing weight and was still eating way too much food. She shared, "I was losing hope about my weight. I was facing menopause, and my metabolism was slowing down. I continued to ask God for help."

Hope For Your Journey

Thankfully, God heard her concerns, and He began to speak to Crystal through other people. Her Heavenly Father provided an "ah ha" moment of clarity and gave her the word "HEALTH." After several "mini miracles," she quickly understood that "HEALTH" encompassed much more than weight loss and good eating habits. God wanted ALL areas of her life to be healthy.

Like a light switch, Crystal realized she had surrendered only parts of her life to God because she did not want to bother Him. It never occurred to her. He wanted to guide ALL areas of her life, including weight loss. He wanted to be Lord over her entire life.

So, with that awareness, Crystal ensured she surrendered all aspects of her life (physical, spiritual, mental, emotional, financial, relationships, job, weight loss, etc.) to God. She stopped looking backward and focused on a 360-degree healthy future as God continued to open new doors.

"Cast your cares on the Lord
and he will sustain you..."
Psalm 55:22 (NIV)

As a benefit of the new company, Crystal received a caring and loving health coach. Together, they established a focused weight loss plan that included increased proteins, reduced carbs, increased healthy fats, and increased fruits and vegetables. Crystal made a mental shift to view "junk food" as poison for her body and finally relinquished her "junk food obsession" to God. She immediately started to lose one to two pounds a week.

Crystal's health coach taught her how to fill the refrigerator/pantry with yummy healthy options and shared recipes to make the transition to healthy eating fun. As Crystal ate the way God intended, pounds continued to "fall off" her small frame, and they celebrated every pound she lost.

As the months passed, Crystal's coach encouraged her to enter the Better Health Challenge, a national contest for weight loss and health. She gladly accepted the challenge, which came with hefty financial awards for the winners. This contest provided additional accountability for Crystal to stay focused and on her HEALTH path.

A Weight Loss Journey – And So Much More

As Crystal's size began to shrink, her company, friends, and family made a "big deal" about her significant weight loss milestones (e.g., 20 / 30 / 40 pounds lost.) Then, finally, she saw 199 pounds on the scale! It was a thrill and a major accomplishment in her journey.

As Crystal continued to lose weight, she began to focus on the broader aspects of HEALTH with the guidance of God and her coach! Before long, she started to exercise and build muscle. As a result, she regained physical stamina. From a spiritual perspective, Crystal prioritized quiet time with God and strived to praise Him for His beautiful creations during neighborhood and nature walks. She was gaining balance and joy in her life.

> *"The light shines in the darkness,*
> *and the darkness has not overcome it."*
> *John 1:5 (NIV)*

Crystal also adjusted her sleep habits to improve her physical, emotional, and mental well-being. She said, "I used to burn the candle at both ends and run on 5-6 hours of sleep daily. I now strive for 7-8 hours of sleep. I feel so much better!" Crystal's "well-rested" body began to pay dividends in all aspects of her life.

Finally, after two years of hard work, it happened. With God's steadfast guidance and support, Crystal lost over eighty pounds and was the Grand Champion for the national "Better Health Challenge." This exciting recognition came with a $5,000 reward. She was thrilled and praised God.

As the various aspects of her life continued to "get healthy," her self-confidence and self-esteem blossomed. Crystal's relationships and interactions with family, friends, and co-workers also improved. She was stronger emotionally, mentally, and socially. It was amazing. She was grateful and openly thanked God at every turn.

But God was not done with Crystal's journey. Through friends and family, her Heavenly Father prompted her to become a Certified Health Coach to help others. Striving to be obedient, she trusted Him and enrolled in a training program. After several months of hard work, Crystal gained valuable coaching skills and became a part-time certified Health Coach. She had no idea her new "coaching skills" were stepping stones for the next chapter in her journey with God.

Hope For Your Journey

For you see, two major aspects of her HEALTH journey still required attention and revitalization. Crystal needed a full-time and profitable job (occupational health) to help plan for her family's future (financial health.) So, once again, God began to whisper to Crystal, and she listened with an open mind. Before long, God created interactions with people who started to point her toward a career in financial planning and advising.

After weeks of listening, praying, and seeking God's will for her career, Crystal suddenly had an unexplained and burning desire to become a financial advisor. Surprisingly, this desire began to make perfect sense.

Crystal had a unique perspective and empathy for people struggling with debt and financial challenges. She had first-hand knowledge about financial hardships during stressful times. She also understood the pitfalls of credit card debt and not following a budget. In addition to her first-hand experiences, God had faithfully equipped her with "coaching skills," the ability to learn quickly, and strong math skills.

God took the various puzzle pieces of Crystal's life and created a clear path for her to achieve this new career goal. He connected her with a well-established Christian-based financial company that fit her personality and values. After numerous interviews and rigorous regulatory tests, Crystal was hired and placed in an intensive training program.

During this same time, God performed another encouraging miracle. Crystal routinely took advantage of grocery store specials for healthy food options. One evening, her grocery cart overflowed with shrimp, chicken, and gluten-free items she planned to freeze for the upcoming month. Crystal anticipated her bill would be approximately $500 as the grocery clerk scanned over a hundred food items.

Just as she inserted her VISA card into the payment machine, the store's IT system lost her entire transaction and began to reboot. After some discussion, the clerk told Crystal, "We are not re-scanning your items. Please consider this a gift from the store." Crystal responded, "Are you kidding me? There is probably $500 worth of food here." The clerk replied, "No, I'm not kidding. Have a good night." Crystal praised God all the way home.

Within less than a year, she became a Financial Advisor. Her clientele quickly expanded thanks to her marketing skills and empathetic coaching. God blessed her with a full-time, profitable job that began to transform her family's financial situation. For you see, with God, all things are possible!

Crystal's story was SO MUCH MORE than a weight-loss journey. She shared, "As I fully surrendered all aspects of my life to my Heavenly Father, He immediately met me right where I was. As I prayed for His guidance and walked in faith, He revitalized me physically, spiritually, mentally, emotionally, socially, financially, and occupationally. He transformed me from the inside out and rebuilt my life one step at a time."

"And God is able to bless you abundantly,
so that in all things at all times, having all that you need,
you will abound in every good work."
2 Corinthians 9:8 (NIV)

Hope For Your Journey

REFLECTION

Are you living all parts of your life with God or trying to accomplish things "on your own."

Take a moment and complete this quick "self-evaluation." As you reflect on the areas outlined below, check your responses.

- **Physically**   With God? _____   On my own? _____

- **Spiritually**   With God? _____   On my own? _____

- **Mentally**   With God? _____   On my own? _____

- **Emotionally**   With God? _____   On my own? _____

- **Socially**   With God? _____   On my own? _____

- **Financially**   With God? _____   On my own? _____

- **Occupationally** With God? _____   On my own? _____

A Weight Loss Journey – And So Much More

NEXT STEPS

God cares about every part of your life.

Is there an area where you need help? Do you want help physically, spiritually, mentally, emotionally, socially, financially, or occupationally? Do you need help in more than one area?

_____

_____

_____

_____

_____

_____

_____

There is good news. God is available 24/7 to listen to your concerns and requests. You can pray this simple prayer:

Dear Heavenly Father,
I am struggling with _____ and _____.
I need your help. I can't do this alone. Thank you. Amen.

CLOSING PRAYER

Dear God,

Thank you for caring about ALL aspects of my life. I want to stop trying to "do life on my own." Please help me trust you with all the parts of my life. Thank you. Amen.

Touching Lives Through Teaching

"For we are God's handiwork,
created in Christ Jesus to do good works,
which God prepared in advance for us to do."
Ephesians 2:10 (NIV)

From an early age, Melanie wanted to be a school teacher. While growing up, she loved "playing school" and helping the neighborhood children with math, reading, and writing. She pretended to lead a class of students and give them various assignments. It was fun and filled her heart with joy. As she continued to grow up, her passion for teaching never disappeared.

When it came time for Melanie to graduate from high school and pursue a college degree, she was confident about her next steps and wanted to become a public school teacher. She aspired to positively impact the lives of elementary children while making their education a fun and rewarding experience. Melanie believed it was God's purpose for her life and was excited about her future.

"For I know the plans I have for you," declares the Lord,
"plans to prosper you and not to harm you,
plans to give you hope and a future."
Jeremiah 29:11 (NIV)

As Melanie graduated from college and ventured into the world with rose-colored glasses, she fully expected to get a teaching position and begin fulfilling her lifetime dream. She initially planned to live with her parents to save money. She had a great relationship with her family and was happy with this decision.

Unfortunately, things did not unfold as Melanie originally hoped. After moving back home, she discovered there were no full-time teaching jobs in the local school district. The lack of a full-time job perplexed her, and she thought, "Why can't I find a teaching job when I'm trying to fulfill God's purpose for my life?"

Surrounded by her parents' wise counsel and support, Melanie prayed for God's guidance. She knew her Heavenly Father had a long-term plan, but she was caught off-guard by the bumps in her path. Reluctantly, Melanie decided to be a substitute teacher while praying for a full-time teaching position. This job was not what she envisioned, but she was grateful for the income and additional teaching experience.

"And we know that in all things God works
for the good of those who love him,
who have been called according to his purpose."
Romans 8:28 (NIV)

It is tough to be a substitute teacher, especially for a new graduate. Each day, Melanie encountered new challenges with a different set of children. However, through this opportunity, she learned to be flexible, creative, and resilient. God used this experience to teach Melanie valuable "real-life" lessons that equipped her with skills and courage for a lifetime.

Fortunately, the following year, Melanie received a full-time, first-grade teaching position at an inner-city school. God answered her prayers, but again, not exactly how she envisioned. Teaching in the inner city would be difficult; however, she trusted God and knew He had a plan.

"Rejoice always, pray continually,
give thanks in all circumstances;
for this is God's will for you in Christ Jesus."
1Thessalonians 5:16-18 (NIV)

As the school year unfolded, Melanie was heartbroken when she discovered the daily hardships many of her little six-year-old students endured. Despite their smiling faces, children came to school in the middle of the winter without breakfast, lunch, or a coat. Some came from broken homes with parents who were alcoholics, on drugs, or in jail. It was gut-wrenching.

Thankfully, God met Melanie every day in the four walls of that little classroom, even on the days when she felt overwhelmed and

Hope For Your Journey

wondered what she was doing. Despite the challenging environment and less-than-desirable work conditions, He quietly encouraged her through the school's teachers and staff. Melanie realized she could make a difference and bring moments of joy to these little children while helping them read and write. She faithfully prayed for her students and their families.

"So do not fear, for I am with you;
do not be dismayed, for I am your God.
I will strengthen you and help you;
I will uphold you with my righteous right hand."
Isaiah 41:10 (NIV)

The following year, Melanie was married and moved to a city in Northern Virginia. She hoped to get a job at one of the best school districts in the country, but no full-time teaching positions were available. She again thought, "Why can't I get a job?" With no other options, she reluctantly accepted an assistant teaching position and continued praying for a full-time teaching position.

Then, one summer day, Melanie felt God prompting her to contact the Washington DC School District and inquire about a full-time teaching position. DC was a thirty-minute commute from her home, so she made a few phone calls. Surprisingly, she landed two interviews.

At the end of the interviews, the principal said, "We want to hire you as a full-time teacher. You can teach any grade you want." Somewhat shocked, Melanie replied, "Hey...I still need to apply for a job at the District Office." Everyone laughed. She knew God was opening doors, and His plan was unfolding.

"Ask and it will be given to you;
seek and you will find;
knock and the door will be opened to you."
Matthew 7:7 (NIV)

That September, Melanie found herself once again teaching in an inner-city school. Only this time, the school was in Southeast DC across from the Navy Yard – one of the city's toughest areas. Her classroom was sparse as it only had desks, a blackboard, and one bulletin board. There were no school supplies, and books were limited. There was a bullet hole in one of her windows. God had been preparing her to teach at this school.

Touching Lives Through Teaching

Melanie had to be innovative to create a positive learning environment for her first grade students. So, after decorating her classroom with bright, cheerful colors, she asked friends and family to donate books for the children to read. Since a solid teaching curriculum did not exist, Melanie made up a curriculum for her class. She could feel God's presence as she tried to figure things out. Thankfully, the principal and teaching staff were very supportive. She was grateful.

The challenges facing Melanie's students were overwhelming. Every day, she did her best to meet the children where they were despite their rough home lives and significant learning problems. On really tough days, she thought, "Why am I worrying? God placed me at this school. I need to remember I can't do this by myself – I don't have to do this by myself. God will help me."

"Cast all your anxiety on him
because he cares for you."
1 Peter 5:7 (NIV)

Melanie continued to feel God's presence as she dealt with a child who was a "selective mute," children with severe learning disabilities, and others with extreme discipline issues. Some kids were hard to reach, but Melanie said, "I tried to make sure each child knew they were loved." Despite the ups and downs, she kept pressing forward and prayed, prayed, prayed!

Amid the obstacles, Melanie strived to make learning fun while teaching the children practical life skills. The kids loved learning math through "Market Days." They used play money to purchase fun books and trinkets. Writing was exciting when the kids submitted "job applications" for the weekly classroom leadership positions, including line leader, office messenger, and official door holder. Reading was entertaining when she dressed in comical outfits and wore fun hats. She brought joy to their lives.

"Let us not become weary in doing good,
for at the proper time we will
reap a harvest if we do not give up."
Galatians 6:9 (NIV)

When Melanie spoke with the children's parents, grandparents, or guardians, she often heard gut-wrenching stories about the severe problems at home, including alcohol, drugs, jail, and poverty. God

Hope For Your Journey

allowed her to "be present" during these tough conversations, listening with compassion and not passing judgment. After discussions, she prayed for the families, then followed up with friendly "check-ins" to offer encouragement. For you see, in addition to helping her students in the classroom, God also used Melanie to support the families of her students.

As a new teacher in Washington, DC, Melanie had the opportunity to receive fifteen free credits from Catholic University – credits that went toward her master's degree in education. In addition, since she taught in the DC Public School District, she had the opportunity to finish her master's degree at a 50% discount. Melanie took full advantage of this unexpected benefit over the next few years.

Due to her relationship with this university, some of Melanie's professors applied for and received a low-income educational grant to procure computers for her elementary school. It was a huge blessing for the students and teachers. She knew it was not a coincidence and thanked God for His intervention.

For seven years, Melanie taught first and second grade in a school and location that was never part of her plan. Through this experience, God kept her safe and expanded her teaching skills as she strived to make a difference. Melanie faithfully prayed and sought God's will as she planted seeds of encouragement and love – the fruits of the Spirit.

"But the fruit of the Spirit is love, joy, peace,
forbearance, kindness, goodness, faithfulness,
gentleness and self-control.

Against such things there is no law."
Galatians 5:22-23 (NIV)

Melanie was particularly thankful for the team she worked with at the school. The principal and teachers encouraged her when she struggled and celebrated when her students overcame learning challenges and achieved new skills. They were an amazing group of people.

However, the significance of this vital support group became crystal clear when Melanie's husband, Steve, was severely injured while performing his duties as a police officer. The teaching staff prayed as her husband fought for his life and rallied around her as she juggled her time between the hospital and teaching responsibilities. Melanie will

Touching Lives Through Teaching

"forever be grateful" for their unconditional love and kindness during this challenging time. Thankfully, after a lengthy rehabilitation process, her husband fully recovered and returned to work.

"My command is this:
Love each other as I have loved you."
John 15:12 (NIV)

Just as seasons change during the year, so do the phases of our lives. While still teaching in DC, God blessed Melanie and her husband with a new baby boy. Around the same time, the principal at her elementary school changed jobs – things were different.

The following summer, her best friend left her teaching job in DC to accept a position in Northern Virginia. Her friend's career change motivated Melanie to re-evaluate her current work location. A teaching position closer to home would be much easier now that she was a mom. Some of the local elementary schools were looking to hire full-time teachers, and she was interested.

Once again, she turned to God and asked for guidance regarding the next steps in her career. Before long, God again opened a new door. She bravely called an elementary school near her house and inquired about teaching positions. Surprisingly, the hiring principal asked her to come for an interview before seeing her resume.

This request caught Melanie off-guard since she did not have a current resume. So, she quickly pulled together some pictures from her prior classes and headed to the interview. After a positive conversation, she was shocked when the principal said, "We want to hire you." Melanie giggled as she once again said, "I still need to apply for a job at the District Office." God was clearly in control and placed her at this school.

"Trust in the Lord with all your heart
and lean not on your own understanding;
in all your ways submit to him,
and he will make your paths straight."
Proverbs 3:5-6 (NIV)

Melanie remained at this school for the next twenty-five years, teaching first and second grade. Every year, she faithfully prayed for her students and their families. When faced with special needs children and other learning challenges, she prayed, "Dear God, I don't know why I am this child's teacher, but whatever my role is in their education, please let me know how I can minister to them."

"May these words of my mouth
and this meditation of my heart
be pleasing in your sight,
Lord, my Rock and my Redeemer."
Psalm 19:14 (NIV)

As Melanie's career progressed, it became clear God also wanted her to support co-workers in various ways. She was grateful for this opportunity to serve God. When we faithfully pursue God's purpose for our lives, He will use us" right where we are" in ways we never imagined.

So, with an open heart, Melanie purposely "hung around" after school each day to visit with the staff and encourage them. She learned some staff members had a relationship with the Lord and others did not, but that never inhibited her conversations. She strived to accept people where they were on their journey and to never "pass judgment."

As Melanie listened to her co-workers, God always opened doors for meaningful conversations. No conversations were "off the table" as they discussed teaching challenges, bad marriages, illnesses, raising children, and losing loved ones. Sometimes, during the discussions, God provided opportunities for Melanie to pray with people, invite them to church, or show them how to read the Bible. She shared, "When people were going through hard times, I could feel God providing me with the right words to say and how to respond to different situations. I was grateful."

"She speaks with wisdom,
and faithful instruction is on her tongue."
Proverbs 31:26 (NIV)

Today, Melanie continues to "live out her faith" while teaching at this same elementary school. She strives to make learning fun while praying for her students and their families. Melanie still plants seeds of faith while encouraging the school staff. To sum it up, she lives in the real world while doing her best to fulfill God's purpose for her life.

Melanie shared, "Teaching in the public schools, like all areas of life, is a mission field filled with hurting people. But there is good news. A

Touching Lives Through Teaching

lot of Christian teachers and administrators are working in our schools. They are faithfully praying for our students and families. It makes a difference!"

She continued, "Yes, we cannot deliver specific messages about the Christian faith in the classroom due to the separation of church and state. However, there continues to be a positive Christian influence in our schools, thanks to our Christian teachers, staff, and principals. Praise God!"

May God bless our public school teachers and the staff who support them. Amen.

Melanie Teaching 2nd Grade

Hope For Your Journey

REFLECTION

1. Throughout Melanie's career, she faithfully trusted God and sought His will. Are you trusting God with your career and seeking His will for your life?

_____

_____

_____

_____

_____

_____

2. Every day after school, Melanie trusted God as she "hung out" to encourage her co-workers and "be available." Can you recall a time when you made yourself available to support and encourage others?

_____

_____

_____

_____

_____

_____

Touching Lives Through Teaching

NEXT STEPS

As we saw in Melanie's story, she prayed throughout the day as she sought God's will. Prayer is the most underutilized power in this world. It is our opportunity to have a conversation with God.

How can you expand your prayer time with our Heavenly Father? Some ideas might include:

- Taking prayer walks
- Praying in your car
- Finding a regular time to pray
- Keeping a prayer journal
- Joining a prayer group
- Getting a prayer partner

CLOSING PRAYER

Dear Heavenly Father,

Thank you for school teachers, administrators, and staff. Please encourage their hearts and keep them safe. Please bless every teacher, administrator, and staff member striving to accomplish YOUR will for our children. I love you. Amen.

The Power of a Simple Apology and Forgiveness

*"...Strive for full restoration, encourage one another,
be of one mind, live in peace.
And the God of love and peace will be with you."
2 Corinthians 13:11 (NIV)*

Brooke was done! The stress of her job in a hostile work environment was intolerable. Finally, after sleepless nights and discussions with her husband, she submitted her resignation and quit. It was no longer possible to work for a demanding perfectionist.

Brooke grew up in a small town where everyone knew each other. After graduating from the local high school, she married, had children, and postponed her dreams of going to college and pursuing a career. She loved being a mother and raising her children, but in the privacy of her home, her controlling husband made life extremely difficult. For years, Brooke suffered in silence as her husband attacked her self-esteem and diminished her self-worth. She tried to maintain a cheerful façade around family and friends but was losing hope.

After her children started school, Brooke found a part-time job to get a break from her caustic home life. The management team quickly recognized her capabilities and recommended classes at the local community college. Despite resistance from home, she decided to take her first college class and received an "A." This success empowered Brooke, who gained enough self-confidence to pursue guidance regarding her hostile home environment. She soon realized there were options, but the road to freedom would not be easy.

*"I can do all things through Christ who strengthens me."
Philippians 4:13 (NKJV)*

Brooke tried to make their marriage work, but her husband's controlling behavior and emotional abuse intensified. She finally realized her husband would not change, and she could no longer live in an oppressive and mentally abusive environment. While she did not have physical scars from her abuse, the mental scars were deep and painful.

After months of prayer, she made the difficult decision to move out and file for divorce, a decision her friends and family failed to understand. Instead of support and empathy, she faced judgment, criticism, and gossip for leaving her marriage. Despite the condemnation, Brooke felt it was the best decision for her family and knew God was with her.

> *"Do not judge, and you will not be judged.*
> *Do not condemn, and you will not be condemned.*
> *Forgive, and you will be forgiven."*
> *Luke 6:37 (NIV)*

Her journey to freedom was not easy. Suddenly, she was a single mom, living in a small apartment and working full-time to make ends meet. At every turn, she faced new challenges. Despite the pressures, she felt a huge sense of relief and continued to trust her Heavenly Father.

Thankfully, Brooke met a caring man who supported her dream of being a great mom while building a career. After a few years, they married and created a loving home for their children. She soon landed a new job while still pursuing her degree from the local community college.

Brooke's self-confidence grew, so she accepted a position with a different company to expand her technical skills. At the new company, she supported a project lead named Ashley, a recent college graduate focused on career advancement. Ashley believed the key to success was working long hours and never asking for help. Failure was not an option.

Brooke's initial working relationship with Ashley was great. They genuinely respected each other, enjoyed working together, and became friends. Their work products generated outstanding customer reviews and attracted new clients. The management team was thrilled.

Unfortunately, as customer accolades grew, Ashley became enthralled with selfish career ambitions. She strived to be the #1 employee at all times. She had grand aspirations to run the local company before she turned forty.

*"Do nothing out of selfish ambition or vain conceit.
Rather, in humility value others above yourselves,
not looking to your own interests
but each of you to the interests of the others."*
Philippians 2:3-4 (NIV)

As project requirements increased, the work environment became very stressful. Ashley failed to ask for additional resources. She thought asking for help was a sign of weakness. So, instead, she kept piling extra work on Brooke with demanding deadlines. Twelve-hour workdays soon became "the norm" for both women. There was no work-life balance.

As pressures mounted, Ashley became demanding and inflexible. She expected perfection and lacked compassion for the unrealistic workload and deadlines. The stressful environment was particularly challenging for Brooke due to her years of emotional and verbal abuse. It re-opened old wounds.

*"Pride goes before destruction,
a haughty spirit before a fall."*
Proverbs 16:18 (NIV)

Unfortunately, due to exhaustion and the demanding working environment, Brooke made a few mistakes that delayed deliverables and upset some customers. Ashley was intolerant of the errors and continued to push for perfection. Finally, fearful for her job, Brooke filed a formal complaint regarding Ashley's unacceptable leadership. Their friendship immediately fractured.

Ashley felt betrayed. She feared Brooke's complaints to management would negatively impact her career aspirations. Despite trying to work through the situation, the remnants of their working relationship collapsed, and their ability to work together became intolerable. Ashley failed to ask for help, management did not intervene, and the unrealistic deadlines continued.

Brooke's health began to deteriorate due to the stressful situation. Finally, after a long discussion with her husband, she submitted her immediate resignation, did not provide two weeks' notice, and packed her things. Ashley was stunned when she saw Brooke carrying her personal items out of the office. She tried to intervene, but it was too late. Brooke was done!

The Power of a Simple Apology and Forgiveness

Suddenly, Ashley was solely responsible for the demanding projects. As a result, despite working from 7 AM to midnight daily (plus weekends), critical deadlines were missed, customers were upset, and management was concerned. Overwhelmed by the situation, Ashley finally realized this was her fault – there was no one else to blame.

> *"When pride comes, then comes disgrace,*
> *but with humility comes wisdom."*
> *Proverbs 11:2 (NIV)*

Somewhere along her career journey, Ashley transitioned her energy, plans, and focus to the world and took her eyes off God. She became consumed by her worldly goal of "climbing the corporate ladder." As a result of her selfish ambitions, Ashley lost a friend and an outstanding technical lead.

The sad fact is that both Ashley and Brooke were Christians. They knew better! They became so focused on the worldly aspects of their situation that they failed to stop and ask God to lead them through their problems.

Ashley felt guilty for her behavior and lack of compassion. What was she going to do? She began to pray about the situation and asked herself, "When did I become so self-centered? Why did I allow the circumstances to spiral out of control? God, what do I need to learn from this mess?"

> *"God, pick up the pieces. Put me back together again.*
> *You are my praise!"*
> *Jeremiah 17:14 (MSG)*

Then, one day, things became clear. Ashley owed Brooke an apology, but she was embarrassed – her pride started to get in the way once again. "What if Brooke does not accept my apology? What if she says I'm an awful person?" Ashley continued to pray and ask God for the courage to apologize. In retrospect, she realized the adversary did not want their relationship restored.

> *"...Be strong and courageous. Do not be afraid;*
> *do not be discouraged, for the Lord your God*
> *will be with you wherever you go."*
> *Joshua 1:9 (NIV)*

Hope For Your Journey

Finally, after several months of "feeling uncomfortable," Ashley prayed, called Brooke, and asked if they could meet for lunch. With some hesitancy, Brooke agreed to meet at a local cafe the next day. Ashley was relieved but was still very nervous.

When they arrived at the restaurant the following day, they politely acknowledged each other and selected their food from the cafeteria-style offerings. Walking together, they chose a table away from the crowd, sat down, and faced each other for the first time in months. It was uncomfortable. As they both removed their food from their trays, Ashley placed her hands on her lap, whispered a short prayer, and said, "Brooke, I owe you an apology. I am sorry for the way I treated you and behaved at work. I am so very sorry."

"Humble yourselves, therefore, under God's mighty hand,
that he may lift you up in due time."
1 Peter 5:6 (NIV)

With that simple yet heart-filled apology, the tensions around the small café table began to melt away, and the restoration of their friendship began. Ashley set aside her ego (Edging God Out) and followed God's promptings to restore their broken relationship – and Brooke gracefully extended the gift of forgiveness. It took some time for Brooke and Ashley to rebuild their trust in each other, but all things are possible with God.

Brooke and her family ironically purchased a home across the street from Ashley the following year. Before long, Brooke and Ashley became close friends, and their families celebrated special occasions together. For you see, God not only restored their friendship, but He enriched it.

"For I know the plans I have for you," declares the Lord,
"plans to prosper you and not to harm you,
plans to give you hope and a future."
Jeremiah 29:11 (NIV)

Ashley's career continued to excel as she put God first. With the help of a Christian executive coach, she transformed into a compassionate, empathetic leader who became a Senior Vice President several years later. She was no longer a self-centered, overbearing project lead but a positive, energetic leader who strived to embrace the "Fruits of the Spirit" in all areas of her life.

*"But the fruit of the Spirit is love, joy, peace,
forbearance, kindness, goodness, faithfulness,
gentleness and self-control.
Against such things there is no law."*
Galatians 5:22-23 (NIV)

After taking a few classes every semester, Brooke finally graduated with a bachelor's degree in business administration. Her strong work ethic and attention to detail propelled her career to positions she never imagined. She was grateful.

In her Senior Vice President role, when Ashley needed a dedicated individual to oversee a critical company-wide certification, her mind immediately turned to Brooke. Ashley offered the position to Brooke, and she accepted without hesitation! God completed the final step of their restoration as they began to work together once again.

Ashley and Brooke helped their team succeed for the next decade as they continued to put God first. They had fun. Their positive working relationship and friendship flourished thanks to a simple apology and the grace of forgiveness. Praise God!

Hope For Your Journey

REFLECTION

1. Ashley became entrapped in her worldly goals to climb the corporate ladder. As a result, she allowed her pride and ego (<u>E</u>dging <u>G</u>od <u>O</u>ut) to drive her actions.

   Has your pride or ego negatively impacted your life?

   _____

   _____

   _____

   _____

   _____

   _____

   _____

2. Has God restored a relationship in your life due to an apology and the power of forgiveness? If yes, what happened?

   _____

   _____

   _____

   _____

   _____

   _____

   _____

The Power of a Simple Apology and Forgiveness

NEXT STEPS

1. Is God prompting you to extend an apology to someone in your life? If yes, ask God to help you find the words and the courage to take the next step. Then, make a call or send a text. Don't wait. Life is too short to live with regrets.

2. Is God prompting you to forgive someone? If yes, ask God to help you with the grace to forgive. He will remove the anger and hurt from your heart – then replace it with His love. God is in the restoration business – trust Him!

CLOSING PRAYER

Dear Heavenly Father,

There are days when I become absorbed with material things, earthly goals, recognition, and status. Please forgive me.

Please lead my actions and heart as I strive to fulfill YOUR purpose for my life. Thank you for guiding my daily steps here on earth.

I love you. Amen.

Pay it Forward

"A generous person will prosper;
whoever refreshes others will be refreshed."
Proverbs 11:25 (NIV)

It was another tough month. Dave was in terrible pain from an unknown illness, and his health continued to deteriorate. After numerous doctor appointments and countless specialized tests, the best doctors in the country were mystified. They were unable to determine a diagnosis.

Erin, Dave's wife, was doing her best to provide full-time home care for her husband while teleworking at least fifty hours a week during the peak of the COVID pandemic. Her faith in God sustained her, but to be honest, some days were overwhelming. She was emotionally and physically exhausted.

"Cast your cares on the Lord
and he will sustain you..."
Psalm 55:22 (NIV)

Then, one cold Saturday in January, she bundled up to run a few errands. On her way home, she thought a surprise might brighten Dave's day, so she placed an order at the Starbucks drive-through. When she approached the window, the cashier kindly said, "The driver in front of you paid for your order. Have a nice day!"

"...In humility value others above yourselves,
not looking to your own interests
but each of you to the interests of the others."
Philippians 2:3-4 (NIV)

When Erin heard the cashier's words, she burst into tears, and her heart was full of gratitude. A stranger extended love and compassion right when she needed it. As she attempted to pull herself together, Erin handed her charge card to the cashier and said, "I want to pay it forward and cover the bill for the car behind me."

Pay it Forward

"Let us not become weary in doing good,
for at the proper time
we will reap a harvest if we do not give up.
Therefore, as we have opportunity,
let us do good to all people..."
Galatians 6:9-10 (NIV)

As Erin drove away, wiping the tears from her eyes, she paused and thanked God for the special person who made her day. She also thanked her Heavenly Father for the daily encouragement and support He provided in big and small ways. She knew God was with her.

Then, with a full and grateful heart, Erin rushed home to share her story with Dave. She also called family and friends to share her special blessing. For you see, this stranger at Starbucks encouraged Erin and Dave and positively touched the lives of everyone who listened to her story.

This small yet significant "pay it forward" moment gave Erin renewed hope as she continued to care for her husband. While she did not know how her husband's story would unfold here on earth, she was thankful for her Heavenly Father's sustaining love and support.

"Be joyful in hope, patient in affliction, faithful in prayer."
Romans 12:12 (NIV)

Hope For Your Journey

REFLECTION

1. Take a deep breath and reflect on your life. When did God use strangers, friends, or family to encourage or help you?

_____

_____

_____

_____

_____

_____

_____

_____

2. What did it feel like when God helped you through other people?

_____

_____

_____

_____

_____

_____

_____

Pay it Forward

NEXT STEPS

Ask God how He can use you to encourage someone this week.

_____

_____

_____

_____

_____

_____

_____

_____

_____

_____

CLOSING PRAYER

Dear Heavenly Father,

I want to help others. Please open my eyes and ears. Show me where and when I can help. Thank you. Amen.

Take Time to Re-Energize

*"Come to me, all you who are weary and
burdened, and I will give you rest."*
Matthew 11:28 (NIV)

Dianne was stressed, and her usual "joyful heart" felt strangled. She was emotionally and physically exhausted as she packed for another business trip. She quickly closed her suitcase before crawling into bed and thought, "Oh dear God, how can I keep pressing forward?"

Over the past year, Dianne faced many challenges. She dealt with health issues while family members encountered unplanned obstacles and friends fought cancer. She also struggled with the pressures of day-to-day life, including financial concerns, volunteer commitments, an aging mother, and the inability to say "no." As a result, she over-committed and strived not to disappoint anyone.

Adding to her stress, Dianne had an ego (Edging God Out) problem. She took pride in being busy with worldly actions and believed slowing down was a sign of weakness. But, deep down, she realized this belief was flawed, and something had to change.

Concentrating on her "to-do" list gave Dianne a sense of accomplishment but kept her from God's purpose for her life. She desired to prioritize her focus on God, but she was too busy. Refocusing required energy and time – and she had another business trip in the morning.

*"In all thy ways acknowledge him,
and he shall direct thy paths."*
Proverbs 3:6 (KJV)

At the sound of her 4 AM alarm, Dianne pulled herself out of bed, showered, dressed, grabbed a power bar, and headed to the airport. By 10 AM, her plane began descending toward Manchester, New Hampshire. Dianne took a moment to gaze out the window and immediately felt a sense of peace throughout her body.

Take Time to Re-Energize

First, she observed the white, puffy clouds floating in the bright blue sky. Then, she noticed the miles and miles of green trees surrounding the glistening ponds and sparkling lakes. It was beautiful. She briefly paused and thanked God for the incredible world He created.

When the plane landed, she rushed to pick up her rental car, quickly drove to her hotel, and promptly settled into her room before making business calls and sending emails. Her unrealistic "to-do" list contained over forty actions she needed to complete. Somehow, she managed to "set herself up" for daily failures due to her unrealistic plans. This approach added to her stress.

Then, Dianne received a text that undermined some plans she made earlier in the week. As she attempted to resolve the minor issue over the phone, her voice began to crack, and her eyes filled with tears. Dianne was caught off-guard by her surprising reaction. As frustration and anxiety consumed her mind, she quickly ended the phone call to compose herself.

She was out of energy and drained. So, suddenly and without hesitation, she quit working, grabbed her keys, stopped for an iced coffee, and headed for the countryside. Within twenty minutes, Dianne could feel her body relaxing as she drove on the country roads, enjoying the beautiful pine trees, meadows, and historic villages. She quietly marveled at God's gift of nature and the peaceful little cottages nestled in the woods.

That evening, she joined some dear friends for dinner overlooking a gorgeous lake. They visited, laughed, and talked about life while Dianne set aside her anxieties. It was a gift from God and exactly what she needed. Love, peace, and kindness surrounded Dianne at the dinner table. She was grateful, and her heart filled with joy for the first time in weeks.

> *"A cheerful heart is good medicine,*
> *but a crushed spirit dries up the bones."*
> *Proverbs 17:22 (NIV)*

The following two days of business strategy meetings were highly productive. Dianne relaxed, offered valued input, and enjoyed the people she had the opportunity to work with. She was grateful.

The next morning, Dianne planned to grab an early breakfast, pack her suitcase, and work in her hotel room before heading to the airport.

Hope For Your Journey

However, God began speaking to her heart as she arranged for a noon check-out. His promptings were clear, and it was a 180-degree departure from Dianne's usual routine, so she paid close attention.

> *"My sheep listen to my voice;*
> *I know them, and they follow me."*
> *John 10:27 (NIV)*

"Why are you sitting in a hotel room working again when you could reenergize and enjoy a beautiful lake only ten minutes away? It's okay to take a break." With that clear message, Dianne shut down her computer, loaded up the car, and headed for the lake, unaware of the transformation God had in store for her.

After a short drive, she pulled up to the lake's shoreline. Dianne silenced her phone and sat quietly in her car, absorbing the tranquil and peaceful setting. The view was stunning. Within minutes, Dianne's concerns and worries disappeared. Instead, she was present and enjoying the special "moment in time."

> *"Now may the Lord of peace himself*
> *give you peace at all times and in every way.*
> *The Lord be with all of you."*
> *2 Thessalonians 3:16 (NIV)*

Then, at God's prompting, she exited her car. At that point, Dianne experienced an unforgettable walk with her Heavenly Father. This walk reset her outlook on life and reenergized her soul. For you see, God met Dianne exactly where she was and provided what she needed – God's peace.

> *"The Lord is my shepherd, I lack nothing.*
> *He makes me lie down in green pastures,*
> *he leads me beside quiet waters,*
> *he refreshes my soul."*
> *Psalm 23:1-3 (NIV)*

As she began walking by the lake, she could feel the cool morning breeze brushing against her face. It was refreshing. Dianne stopped, closed her eyes, and took several deep breaths of God's revitalizing air. She thanked Him for the air she was breathing before moving on.

Dianne paused and reflected on a fact she had known all her life, "I cannot see the air, but it keeps me alive. Just like God, I cannot see

Take Time to Re-Energize

Him, but He is always with me." Then, she whispered, "Thank you, God. I love you!"

> *"...And surely I am with you always,*
> *to the very end of the age."*
> Matthew 28:20 (NIV)

God now had Dianne's undivided attention as He unveiled many simple yet profound blessings that reenergized her mind and body. He shared another part of His amazing creation every few steps along her path.

Dianne stopped momentarily at the base of some towering pine trees and marveled at the intricate pinecones God was forming on the branches. As she glanced at the tops of the trees, she observed a few wispy clouds that God had placed in the vibrant blue sky. She quietly watched birds gently gliding in the air as the cool breeze tousled her hair.

A few more steps unveiled beautiful flowers blooming on the trees and delicate wildflowers scattered throughout the grass. The spring colors were stunning and reminded Dianne of new beginnings. The incredible details God designed for each flower were astonishing.

Then, Dianne gazed across the lake and noticed the sun glistening on the water. There was a beautiful mountain in the distance. Suddenly, a fish jumped up and splashed. Dianne smiled and thought, "If God cares enough to handle all the intricacies in nature, why do I fret and worry about my commitments and ridiculous "to-do" lists? God will always guide my path if I ask Him to lead the way."

As she approached some large rocks, she observed some pesky weeds trying to grow between the boulders. She smiled and remembered the Bible story she learned in Sunday School about building your house (life) on the rock (God). God will protect you when Satan (the weeds) come lurking around. She realized the adversary wanted her to be stressed and full of anxiety, thus distracting her from spending quality time with her Heavenly Father each day.

When Dianne circled back to her car, there were some inviting benches by the shore. As she came closer, a small sparrow jumped from the ground to the bench, then back to the ground. It was as if the sparrow was saying, "Come sit with me for a while." As Dianne approached the bench,

Hope For Your Journey

she smiled and thought, "Yes, if I would calmly sit with God every day before tackling my worldly commitments, life would be SO much easier."

As she peacefully sat on the bench, she continued to watch the little sparrow hopping on the ground. Then, she remembered one of her grandfather's favorite hymns, "His Eye is On the Sparrow," based on the following Bible verses:

"Look at the birds of the air;
they do not sow or reap or store away in barns,
and yet your heavenly Father feeds them.

Are you not much more valuable than they?
Can any one of you by worrying
add a single hour to your life?"
Matthew 6:26-27 (NIV)

As Dianne's time at the lake ended, she was grateful God met her right where she was. She chose to slow down and prioritize her time with our Heavenly Father. As a result, He faithfully re-energized her heart, body, and outlook on life.

"Trust in the Lord with all your heart
and lean not on your own understanding;
in all your ways submit to him,
and he will make your paths straight."
Proverbs 3:5-6 (NIV)

Take Time to Re-Energize

REFLECTION

1. Are you exhausted or overwhelmed? What is going on?

    _____

    _____

    _____

    _____

2. We do not need to face our issues, concerns, or anxieties alone. God promises to help us with our challenges, whether big or small.

    "For I am the Lord your God
    who takes hold of your right hand
    and says to you, Do not fear; I will help you."
    Isaiah 41:13 (NIV)

    Do you want or need God's help today?

Hope For Your Journey

NEXT STEPS

1. How can you re-energize today? Some ideas might include:

   - Asking God to re-energize you
   - Taking a walk
   - Thanking God for your blessings
   - Sipping iced tea in a park
   - Having lunch with a friend
   - Turning off the TV and phone
   - Calling a friend
   - Reading the Bible
   - Going to the beach
   - Sitting by a lake or river
   - Watching a sunrise/sunset
   - Playing board games
   - Taking a nap
   - Reading a book

2. What are some steps you can take to ensure you are making God a priority in your life?

   _____

   _____

   _____

   _____

CLOSING PRAYER

Dear Heavenly Father,

Thank you for loving me and caring about the big and little issues in my life. Please help me to keep my priorities straight as I strive to fulfill your purpose for my life. I love you. Amen.

A Final Reflection

"Be joyful in hope, patient in affliction,
faithful in prayer."
Romans 12:12 (NIV)

We live in a fallen world and will face rough times, from choppy waves to dangerous tides and sometimes even tsunamis. Thankfully, there is good news! There is "hope for your journey."

Remember, God loves you regardless of your mistakes, regrets, addictions, bad decisions, and failures. He promises to carry you through the storms of life!

When you trust God, He will sustain you and give you hope. For with God, ALL things are possible!

"Now faith is confidence in what we hope for
and assurance about what we do not see."
Hebrews 11:1 (NIV)

Three Steps to Salvation

If you are interested in real victory –
a personal relationship with God,
follow the steps below.

1. Get Ready…
Admit you have sinned. Tell God what you have done, be sorry for it, and be willing to quit.

"For all have sinned and fall short of the glory of God."
Romans 3:23 (NIV)

2. Get Set…
Believe God loves you and sent His Son, Jesus, to save you from your sins. Accept the forgiveness God offers you.

"For God so loved the world that he gave his one and only Son, that whoever believes in Him shall not perish, but have eternal life." John 3:16 (NIV)

3. Go!
Claim Jesus as your Savior. Acknowledge God's forgiveness, respond with love, and follow Jesus.

"Everyone who calls on the name of the Lord will be saved." Romans 10:13 (NIV)

Share your victory with a friend as you begin your new journey.

© Church of the Nazarene 2018 (Used by Permission)

Milton Keynes UK
Ingram Content Group UK Ltd.
UKHW020947041024
449263UK00011B/665